BEHIND THE SCENES IN LOS ANGELES

A POP CULTURE HISTORY TOUR

ADAM PAPAGAN

THE History PRESS

Published by The History Press
Charleston, SC
www.historypress.com

First published 2025

Manufactured in the United States

ISBN 9781467159210

Library of Congress Control Number: 2025933737

CONTENTS

INTRODUCTION

Although I have only been a tour guide since 2016, I've always been the person friends trust to show *their* guests around town. I am fascinated with pop culture and history and can't think of a better place to grow up. You've got to love your hometown, and I take pride in all the notable things that have happened in Southern California. LA history is world history!

Since turning pro, I've given more than two thousand sightseeing tours and met people from all over the world. People tend to come to Los Angeles with a lot of expectations since they've been hearing about it through the movies or on the news their entire lives. It isn't all swimming pools and movie stars, but it isn't all pollution and traffic either. I see my job as a tour guide as someone who can interpret the city for visitors so they come away with positive feelings about the place.

I have tried to include everything I've ever pointed out or been asked about in a tour. This is not a definitive list of Los Angeles attractions, nor is it even a complete history of them. These are simply the anecdotes I would tell you if we were on a tour in person. I've included a little of everything: movie locations, dining, museums, true crime, infrastructure and good old-fashioned gossip—everything that makes Los Angeles what it is. I've also included some insider tips regarding parking and the best time of day to go, plus a few little stories about people I've met along the way.

Chapter 1

NOTABLE STREETS AND NEIGHBORHOODS

Before we get into this adventure, let me give you the lay of the land. When people think of Los Angeles, what comes to mind is actually Los Angeles County, not just the city of Los Angeles. LA County is made up of a staggering eighty-eight independent cities. Beginning in the mid-twentieth century, a series of loopholes and deregulations allowed areas to incorporate as their own cities with their own laws but contract with the county for things like the fire and police departments at a subsidized rate. Many of these cities have enacted laws to limit what type and how much housing could be built, thus creating an intentional housing shortage that keeps real estate prices high. That's the reason everything is so crazy and expensive here—the county has lacked any meaningful region-wide planning for most of its history.

Most of the city's most popular tourist attractions are located in the central area clustered around the Santa Monica Mountains. These are the areas that tend to pop up most often on television and in popular culture, and many people, even those who live here, never venture into the sprawling suburbs beyond. This chapter primarily covers those main areas and neighborhoods, but there're eighty-some other cities just waiting to be explored on your own.

Olvera Street

845 North Alameda Street, Los Angeles, CA 90012

Historic square turned historic tourist attraction.

It's hard to believe that all that's left of the original Los Angeles is a few blocks north of the 101 Freeway. Although Los Angeles was founded in 1781, the oldest remaining part of the city is Los Angeles Plaza, established in the early 1820s when LA was still a part of Mexico. This was the city's central square, and the area was home to a diverse population of Mexican, American, Italian, French, African and Chinese settlers. The neighborhood was neglected as economic and social life shifted south to LA's growing downtown. When Olvera Street was threatened with demolition in the 1920s, a socialite named Christine Sterling stepped in with a campaign to help preserve some of the buildings. Eventually, a plan was hatched to turn the area into a tourist attraction resembling a "traditional" Mexican marketplace, and that's how it has remained since 1930. Although this romanticized version of Mexico is far from authentic, there's a fakeness about it that's very true to LA's spirit. Just off the central plaza is a plaque commemorating the pobladores, the original Spanish Mexican settlers of Los Angeles. Their names and ages are listed, as well as their European,

The Los Angeles Plaza, depicted in an early postcard. *Detroit Publishing Company.*

African and Native ancestries, highlighting how Los Angeles has always been a diverse place to put down roots.

BEST TIME TO GO: Midday. Merchants close up around sundown.
PARKING: There are exactly three free parking spaces on Alameda. Other than that, try one of the lots across the street.

Angelino Heights

Carroll Avenue and Edgeware Road in Echo Park

Neighborhood of historic Victorian homes, with many featured in movies and TV.

Angelino Heights, one of LA's oldest neighbors, is a quaint collection of preserved Victorian and Queen Anne houses just off the beaten path in Echo Park. Many of the homes date back to the late 1800s, which is practically ancient in Los Angeles terms. Due to its architectural character, Angelino Heights often stands in for San Francisco as a filming location. The area was Los Angeles' first recognized historic district, and they don't skimp on the charm. In fact, the television series *Charmed* was filmed at the Sanders House at 1345 Carroll Avenue, which, prior to that, was featured in the Michael Jackson video for "Thriller." These are private residences; please do not disturb occupants.

BEST TIME TO GO: Easiest to see and appreciate the historic houses during the day.
PARKING: Street parking.

Echo Park

751 Echo Park Avenue, Los Angeles, CA 90026

Community hub with history of eccentric characters.

Echo Park is one of LA's oldest neighborhoods, and its eponymous lake and park have been at the core of the community since the beginning. Before Hollywood really got going, Echo Park was the epicenter of silent-era filmmaking. The first pie-in-the-face gag was filmed at Mack Sennett Studios on what is now Glendale Boulevard. Evangelist Aimee Semple McPherson founded her Angeles Temple (purported to be the world's first megachurch) at the north end of the park. Sister Aimee later created a huge scandal by faking her own disappearance, which resulted in the death of a member of the search party. In the middle of the lake, there is a small plot of land that stands in for an "uncharted desert isle" in exterior shots for *Gilligan's Island*. The neighborhood has had its ups and downs but is today once again the home of creative types and colorful local characters, not unlike the Echo Park of the past.

BEST TIME TO GO: During the day for park vibes, although a twilight cruise in a swan boat can be enchanting.
PARKING: There's a tiny parking lot at the north end of the park, but street parking is easily available.

Hollywood

Between Crescent Heights and Gower

Legendary district of fame, fortune and tragedy.

A few notes on Hollywood, as it is the most visited place in Southern California aside from Disneyland. Hollywood is three things: it is a physical neighborhood in the city of Los Angeles, it is a term for the entertainment industry and it's a state of mind. As a neighborhood with its decaying buildings, souvenir shops and homeless encampments, Hollywood is not quite the playground for movie stars envisioned by most tourists. Travel a little to the north on Cahuenga to Burbank, and you'll find that much of Hollywood the Industry isn't even located in Hollywood proper. But as a feeling, Hollywood is everything it claims to be. This is a place of excitement and unpredictability. It's a place where chance encounters and a little luck can lead to your dreams literally coming true; despite the many, many cautionary tales of tragedy that befall those who have "made it," people still come from all over the world to be part of Hollywood. Few places have had such an impact on the modern psyche, so you should probably try to see it while you're here.

BEST TIME TO GO: There's always something to see in Hollywood.
PARKING: There's always parking in the residential neighborhood east of La Brea.

Hollywood and Vine

The name says it all.

Los Angeles' most famous intersection.

The intersection of Hollywood and Vine was once the epicenter of the Hollywood film industry. *Carol Highsmith.*

Many know Hollywood and Vine as the most famous intersection in entertainment, but most aren't really sure why. During the Golden Age of Hollywood, many radio and movie companies were concentrated around the intersection of Hollywood Boulevard and Vine Street. Radio station KFWB led off its broadcasts with "Live from Hollywood and Vine," and the area was regularly mentioned in newspaper gossip columns as a place of action. Before long, Hollywood and Vine became a symbol of the vortex that lured dreamers to Hollywood. In recent years, the city has installed a diagonal "scramble" crosswalk so you're actually able to stand in the exact center of everything before the light changes. In the modern era, the only major entertainment company still located at the intersection is Capitol Records. However, on the southeastern corner at 1600 Vine is a mixed-use development with a brunch place, a Trader Joe's and luxury apartments popular with YouTubers and social media influencers. It turns out that the next generation of entertainers are still drawn to Hollywood and Vine all these years later.

BEST TIME TO GO: Great people watching at rush hour.
PARKING: You can usually get lucky with a meter a little west of Vine.

Sunset and Vine

The intersection of Sunset Boulevard and Vine Street

Thoroughfare that served as setting for many notable entertainment events.

Although not as famous as the intersection of Hollywood and Vine up the street, the four corners of Sunset and Vine have seen a huge share of entertainment history. The northeast corner was the original site of Cecil B. DeMille and Jesse Lasky's barn, which was used to film *The Squaw Man*, considered the first feature film shot in Los Angeles. Today, it is a bank featuring an ornate tile mosaic depicting Hollywood history. Now long gone, the northwest corner was the former location of NBC Studios before it moved to Burbank. Moving south, the southeast corner is the location of the Cinerama Dome, maybe the second-most famous movie theater in the world after the Chinese Theater. Just off the southeast corner was the Aquarius Theater, which was recently repainted with psychedelic murals to appear as it did in the 1960s, when acid-fueled rock bands performed there. Sunset and Vine is proof that in Hollywood something notable probably happened any place you look.

BEST TIME TO GO: No best time, no worst time.
PARKING: At certain times of day, you can find a meter easily, but this is a drive-by.

Laurel Canyon

Laurel Canyon Boulevard between Hollywood and Mulholland

Canyon community known for hippie history.

In the '60s and '70s, Laurel Canyon was the epicenter of the folk rock and psychedelic rock scenes. Situated just beyond the Sunset Strip, the secluded canyon was home to rock stars such as the Turtles, Love, Carole King, the Eagles, the Byrds, Neil Young and the Mamas and the Papas. The home Joni Mitchell sang of in "Our House" is located in the canyon, and apparently Joni still owns it. There's not really much to stop and explore except for the Canyon Store, which sells munchies and sandwiches as well as overpriced classic rock vinyl, but driving through the hills of Kirkwood and Lookout Mountain, you can still sense the magic that attracted all of these great artists.

BEST TIME TO GO: During the day; there's not much to see at night.
PARKING: There are few places to park or pull over, so you definitely need your own car for this one.

Melrose and Fairfax

Melrose Avenue and Fairfax Avenue

Once and future home of hip fashion and streetwear.

Melrose Avenue and the adjacent Fairfax are known for many boutiques selling sneakers and streetwear. *Carol Highsmith.*

The neighborhood, centered roughly on the intersection of Melrose and Fairfax, is perennially one of the trendiest shopping districts in town. Melrose first rose to prominence in the 1980s as the go-to spot for punk and new wave clothing. In the '90s, the area became a household name due to the success of the show *Melrose Place*. The adjacent Fairfax District was traditionally a heavily Jewish area but, over the years, gave way to a number of sneaker, skateboarding and streetwear shops. Each Sunday, Fairfax High School holds the slightly overpriced Melrose Trading Post swap meet, where you can shop the hottest trends just before they hit the mainstream. At the time of this writing, many boutiques on Melrose are stocking ironic and non-ironic vintage band T-shirts and "exotic" regional sodas and snack foods from around the world. Who knows what will catch on next, but when it does, you know you'll be able to find it on Melrose.

BEST TIME TO GO: Weirdly for a trendy area, everything pretty much closes up by sundown.

PARKING: Street parking in the residential neighborhood, but only for two hours.

The Sunset Strip

Sunset Boulevard between Doheny and Crescent Heights

Glitzy stretch known for billboards and nightlife.

The Sunset Strip has been a playground for the rich and famous since its inception. Prior to becoming part of the city of West Hollywood in 1984, the

Strip was located in an unincorporated area of Los Angeles County, making it a wild, less regulated district outside the jurisdiction of the LAPD just a few blocks over. The fact that it was right between Hollywood and Beverly Hills also made it an ideal place to party. From the '20s to the '50s, it was popular with movie people, who gave way to counterculture and music types from the '60s to the '80s. The area is still known for its many night spots, comedy clubs, hotels, restaurants and enormous billboards, said to be some of the most expensive in the world. The many stories and associations with the Sunset Strip—Van Halen, Bugsy Siegel, *The Rocky Horror Picture Show*, *Selling Sunset*—are endless. It's remarkable to think of all of the layers of pop culture history existing on top of one another in this same space.

The Sunset Strip is known for its many nightclubs and music venues. *Carol Highsmith.*

BEST TIME TO GO: I like to walk the Strip at sunset when the weather cools off. The street is gridlocked with traffic, but you'll have the sidewalk to yourself.

PARKING: There are two public pay lots on the northern side of the street near Holloway and La Cienega, respectively. Sometimes you can snag a meter. Most establishments have their own (paid) parking lots.

Bel Air

Sunset Boulevard to the south, Mulholland Drive to the north, Beverly Glen Boulevard to the east and Sepulveda Boulevard to the west

Exclusive enclave for the famous and powerful containing some of the most expensive houses in the world.

For those of us who live here, it's easy to be desensitized to the sheer amount of wealth concentrated in the hills of Los Angeles. Bel Air is one of the country's most exclusive and expensive neighborhoods, with several homes valued at more than $120 million. Famous residents have included Elon Musk, Ronald Reagan, Beyoncé and many members of the international "1 percent." Many of the homes remain unoccupied for much of the year, serving primarily as real estate investments. If you have a car, it's absolutely worth it to take a drive through the Bel Air gates (it's a public street, so they don't actually shut) to explore and marvel at the unbridled excess of it all. Private residences—please do not disturb occupants.

BEST TIME TO GO: The houses are notoriously hard to see behind the gates as it is, so that's more of a daytime endeavor. The top of the hill has a spectacular view day or night.
PARKING: Perhaps not surprisingly, there is virtually no street parking in Bel Air, and the hills and lack of sidewalks make it inhospitable to pedestrians.

Compton

South of Downtown LA

The birthplace of Southern California hip hop, just outside the city.

The two Los Angeles neighborhoods people always have questions about are Beverly Hills and Compton. It seems the two things the world knows us for are extreme wealth and excess and extreme poverty and violence. In actuality, the city of Compton made famous as the birthplace of gangsta rap by groups like N.W.A is a fairly average but underinvested working-class neighborhood. LA Hood Life Tours gives excellent sightseeing tours of the area that are filled with local insight. Even if you think you're not into hip hop, the story of the music and art that came out of South Central is just as much a part of LA history as William Mulholland or Marilyn Monroe. Scan the radio and you will inevitably land on a song by Snoop Dogg, Tupac, Kendrick Lamar and more—evidence of Compton's continuing contribution to popular culture.

As of 2019, Compton now has an LGBTQ+ Pride festival every year that is usually held in July.

BEST TIME TO GO: Daytime.
PARKING: You can pretty much pull over anywhere.

Century City

10250 Santa Monica Boulevard, Los Angeles, CA 90067

Former studio lot now home to luxury shopping and offices.

According to Tom Petty, Century City is where all the lawyers live. The dense collection of modern office towers and shopping centers just west of Beverly Hills was built on the former backlot of 20th Century Fox. After a string of box office flops culminating with Richard Burton and Elizabeth Taylor's *Cleopatra*, the studio was forced to sell off much of its land, and a business district was developed here in 1963. Fox Studio still stands at the southern edge of the area, but there are also numerous office buildings filled with lawyers, finance and entertainment professionals, as well as a fancy mall where you just might see a celebrity. One of the most recognizable buildings is Fox Plaza, which portrayed Nakatomi Tower in *Die Hard*.

BEST TIME TO GO: During the day. It basically shuts down at night.
PARKING: Park at the mall.

Little Tokyo

Central Avenue and First Street

Historic Japanese neighborhood with modern boutiques and restaurants.

One cool thing about Los Angeles is that it's like being in fifty different countries at once. We're lucky enough to have Chinatown, Koreatown, Little Ethiopia and many other international neighborhoods that allow us to experience the diversity of the world right here in Los Angeles. Little Tokyo is a traditionally Japanese American neighborhood in Downtown Los Angeles and the cultural center for Japanese Americans in Southern California. The area initially began attracting Japanese immigrants in the early twentieth century, but most were forced to leave during the Japanese internment of World War II. A major redevelopment occurred in the '70s and '80s, and now the area resembles an outdoor mall with a plethora of boutiques, restaurants, vintage clothing stores and galleries. There are also several outposts of well-known Japanese chains like

Little Tokyo is home to many legacy businesses and restaurants. *Lee Russel.*

Kinokuniya bookstore. The BYOB karaoke rooms in the mall are also a popular birthday party location.

BEST TIME TO GO: Around lunch or dinner. It's a great place to eat.
PARKING: You can usually find a meter if you drive around long enough.

MALIBU

Pacific Coast Highway (beginning near Sunset Boulevard)

Coastal city known for beach life and celebrity hijinks.

Malibu is a coastal community running north up the Pacific Coast Highway on the western edge of Los Angeles. The area is known for its scenic beauty, surf spots and numerous famous and affluent residents. Although the views are picturesque, there's not a lot to do here besides lie on the beach or get a bite to eat at one of Malibu's many restaurants. Some of my favorite beaches, including Point Dume and El Matador (featured in *Planet of the*

Apes and *Grease*, respectively), are in Malibu, so if you're willing to do a little extra driving, this is a good option for your beach day. The Malibu Village shopping center is the de facto center of social life in Malibu and is another one of those places where you may get a celebrity sighting. Other things Malibu is known for are Mel Gibson's 2006 DUI arrest and anti-Semitic tirade, residents illegally blocking access to public beaches and a McDonald's across the street from the trendy restaurant Nobu where people eat after going to Nobu because the portions are so small. The area is also highly susceptible to wildfires, so go see it before it inevitably burns again.

BEST TIME TO GO: The coast can be overcast in the morning, especially in summer months, but you can't beat Malibu for sunset.
PARKING: Surprisingly a lot of free parking along PCH if you want to jump out for a view of the water.

KOREATOWN

8th Street and Irolo Street

Thriving immigrant neighborhood known for food and international imports.

LA tends to close up rather early for an international, world-class city. Sure, you can always find a late-night taco, but if you're looking for happening restaurants with authentic food, head down to Koreatown. The neighborhood is named for the many Korean immigrants who began settling here in the 1960s. Restaurants serving classic Korean fare like bibimbap and bulgogi, as well as the latest food trends from the streets of Seoul, are plentiful. There are also numerous malls in the area with entire stores dedicated to K-pop music and memorabilia, and more with imported skin care and electronics. The neighborhood is also centrally located with some of the highest housing density in the city, so it's also home to people from all over. Koreatown is a microcosm of the blending of cultures for which Los Angeles is famous.

BEST TIME TO GO: Many of the restaurants are open late.
PARKING: Notoriously difficult, but you may get lucky with a meter. Otherwise, there are numerous pay lots around.

Griffith Park

4730 Crystal Springs Drive, Los Angeles, CA 90027

Large urban park with hiking and attractions.

The observatory gets all the attention, but here is the real story of Griffith J. Griffith. Griffith Park was developed on the site of an old ostrich farm by mining tycoon Colonel Griffith Jenkins Griffith in order to lure residents to his nearby property developments. It was officially donated to the city in 1896. A few years later, Griffith was tried and convicted of shooting and severely wounding his wife while in a drunken rage. After his release from San Quentin in 1906, Griffith attempted to rehabilitate his image by donating much of his large fortune to improvements for the park. The city initially refused but changed its tune after his death and began construction of the observatory and Greek Theater. Today, Griffith Park is the second-largest urban park in the country and a popular recreation area for locals. Attractions found in the park include Griffith Observatory, the Autry Museum of the American West, the Los Angeles Zoo and the Hollywood Sign. The park remains one of the busiest filming locations in Los Angeles. Its credits are too numerous to list, but they go all the way back to the landmark but highly problematic *Birth of a Nation* in 1915. These days, few remember Colonel Griffith and the scandal that sent him to jail, but everyone is able to enjoy the park.

Griffith Park is the nation's largest urban park completely surrounded by one city. *Adam Papagan.*

BEST TIME TO GO: It's nicest the first half of the day before it gets too hot.
PARKING: Free parking throughout the park.

Mulholland Drive

Runs roughly from the Cahuenga Pass to the Sepulveda Pass

Scenic highway with celebrity addresses.

The hills are the most desirable place to live in Los Angeles. Although the houses are crammed together as close as possible (often teetering over cliffs), the hills provide an illusion of privacy and being a world apart from the troubles of the city. Running nearly the entire length of the crest of the Hollywood Hills is Mulholland Drive. The street is named for self-taught civil engineer William Mulholland, who oversaw the construction of the Los Angeles Aqueduct. The innovative infrastructure totally transformed the region, allowing for explosive population growth. He was also responsible for the career-ending collapse of the St. Francis Dam, which killed more than sixty people. Today, Mulholland is mostly remembered for the scenic route that bears his name. The road is a popular settlement for celebrities and is home to everyone from Jack Nicholson to Paul Stanley to Lisa Vanderpump.

BEST TIME TO GO: Take a drive midafternoon but watch out for open-air tour buses blocking the road.
PARKING: There are a few scenic overlooks featuring panoramic views of the San Fernando Valley.

Venice Boardwalk

On the beach roughly between Marina Del Rey and Santa Monica

Seaside tourist trap with abundance of artists and street entertainers.

Venice Beach is one of the best places to people watch in the city. The two-mile stretch along the beach is packed with street entertainers, vendors, roller skaters, bodybuilders and just about every other type of attention seeker. The original Muscle Beach was down at the Santa Monica Pier, but the one that relocated here is where Arnold Schwarzenegger got his start as a weightlifter before becoming an international movie star and later governor of California. It's just a good excuse to be by the beach and see some interesting stuff. Venice is in the midst of yet another wave of gentrification, but there's a layer of bohemian grime there that no amount of fancy coffee will ever be able to get off.

BEST TIME TO GO: I try to get it out of the way in the morning before it gets too crowded, but the afternoons are more lively.
PARKING: I've always had luck on Windward Avenue.

CHINATOWN

Between Broadway and Hill

Kitschy pagodas with new and old school shopping and dining.

When Los Angeles' original Chinatown was demolished to make way for Union Station, community groups got together to create something more fanciful and attractive to tourists. Unlike the Chinatowns in places like San Francisco and New York, LA's Chinatown was designed by Hollywood set designers to create an especially imaginative atmosphere. Brightly colored pagodas mix with more modern commercial buildings and souvenir shops. Many legacy businesses have been in operation from the beginning, including Phoenix Bakery and Yang Chow. Today, the area still serves an aging Chinese population but has also become an innovative art and dining destination. Make sure to grab a picture with the larger-than-life Bruce Lee statue, the only one in North America.

BEST TIME TO GO: Stuff starts to close around sundown.
PARKING: Metered street parking and pay lots.

UNIVERSAL CITY OVERLOOK

7701 Mulholland Drive, Los Angeles, CA 90046

Panoramic views of the Valley well known to tour guides.

The twisting and turning Mulholland Drive offers many opportunities to pull over and enjoy the view, but the one most favored by LA tour guides is the Universal City Overlook. Located toward the eastern end of Mulholland, the

The Universal City Overlook provides a bird's-eye view of many of the area film studios and media companies. *Adam Papagan.*

overlook offers unobstructed views of much of the San Fernando Valley and its most famous entertainment landmarks. From the perch, you see Universal Studios (both the movie studio and the theme park), Warner Bros., Disney, DreamWorks, the former location of NBC and the Hollywood Burbank Airport. A handy placard makes it easy to identify what's what. Seeing these landmarks from afar helps put LA's immense sprawl into perspective and makes you realize that much of what we consider "Hollywood" is actually the Valley.

BEST TIME TO GO: Closes after sundown.
PARKING: It has a few parking spots, so you just pull in.

Chapter 2

BUILDINGS AND INFRASTRUCTURE

When I look at old pictures of Los Angeles, I'm struck not by how much it's changed, but how *little* it's changed. Periodically, a new office or apartment tower will shake up the city's skyline, but whole blocks of houses and shopping centers will go untouched for decades. Individual businesses will come and go, and sure we lose a few local institutions a year, but for the most part many of the buildings that were here in the '20s and '30s are still here today. In a town where fortunes are made and lost and people constantly drift in and out, these structures become not just local landmarks but symbols of stability. They are our meeting places, settings for of our stories and containers for memories. It's a tough town, but the city can also be your friend, reminding you of who you were, who you are now and maybe where you're going next.

The Hollywood Sign

Mount Lee in Beachwood Canyon

The nine magic letters that say so much.

The Hollywood Sign is one attraction that puts a smile on everyone's face. The story of the most famous sign in the world goes back to 1923. The original sign was an advertisement for the planned Hollywoodland neighborhood. The real estate company put up big letters that flashed "HOLLY-WOOD-LAND" to lure prospective buyers. This was somewhat of a common advertising practice at the time, and the hills of Southern California were once scattered with many of these large temporary billboards for the places they would become. Although never meant to be permanent, the Hollywoodland Sign instantly had a certain bit of magic to it. It soon began appearing in films and on postcards, which gave the sign international exposure. Only a few of the original Hollywoodland homes were ever built before the stock market crash of 1929. The company went out of business, leaving the sign untouched for the next twenty years.

In 1949, the Hollywood Chamber of Commerce sponsored the first major refurbishment of the sign, removing the "LAND" part so visitors would associate it more closely with the neighborhood of Hollywood. However, deterioration persisted for decades since this original sign was never meant to be around long. By the 1970s, the Hollywood Sign was in rough shape. The wooden letters were splintering and falling over, and the sign was a regular target of vandals. Something had to be done, so a group of celebrities led by Hugh Hefner got together for a fundraiser at the Playboy Mansion to create a new, permanent steel sign. That's the sign we have today. Take the time to hike all the way to the top and you will hear every language in the world spoken like some sort of Tower of Babel. It seems people from around the globe are compelled to travel to Los Angeles, drive into the hills and make the two-hour trek up the mountain just to be close to this famous sign. It's

The current iteration of the Hollywood Sign was constructed in 1978. *Carol Highsmith.*

not stylized, and it doesn't even light up anymore, but everyone knows it stands for glamour, excitement and all the things that have been drawing people here from the beginning. Naturally, Hollywood's most quintessential landmark is an advertisement for itself.

BEST TIME TO GO: If you're going to hike up there, go in the morning before it gets too hot.
PARKING: Lake Hollywood Park has easy street parking and good views of the sign.

Los Angeles City Hall

200 North Spring Street, Los Angeles, CA 90012

Government building that also plays one on TV.

In LA, even the municipal buildings are stars. Los Angeles City Hall is the headquarters of LA city government but has also been used as a high-profile filming location for many films and TV shows. The building played itself on the classic procedural *Dragnet* and also featured in *War of the Worlds*, *Perry Mason* and *L.A. Confidential* and subbed as the home of the *Daily Planet* in *The Adventures of Superman*. Due to height restrictions, city hall was the tallest building in Los Angeles until 1964, but today it shrinks among the much taller modern office towers surrounding it. The observation deck at the top sports 360-degree views of Downtown Los Angeles and is usually deserted.

BEST TIME TO GO: The observation deck is open Monday through Friday.
PARKING: There are city-run lots in the area, but they can get pricey. If you're already parked downtown, consider walking over.

Santa Monica Pier

200 Santa Monica Pier, Santa Monica, CA 90401

An amusement park with views of the coast.

Some people come to LA and never see the ocean. The Santa Monica Pier is a quick and easy way to experience the ocean if you're short on time.

Sport fishermen can still be found at the end of Santa Monica Pier. *John Margolis.*

The pier's history is pretty typical for an amusement pier of its era. It was built just after the turn of the twentieth century and had various periods of popularity and decline before becoming the pier we have today. There's an old arcade, an older carousel and a newer roller coaster and Ferris wheel that are part of the Pacific Park amusement park. There are also plenty of souvenir stores, tacky (in a good way) restaurants and street entertainers. Since it's by the beach, the vibe here is much chiller than Beverly Hills or Hollywood Boulevard. You could spend a few hours here or just pop in to get a picture of the California coastline.

BEST TIME TO GO: The beaches can be foggy in the morning so check the forecast if you're planning on heading out early. Sunsets are crowded but beautiful.

PARKING: This is probably the best parking tip in this entire book. There's a lot at the foot of the pier on the southern end off Appian Way and Seaside Terrace. If you want to look it up, it's called SP+ Parking on Google. Parking is a dollar or two per hour.

Crossroads of the World

6671 Sunset Boulevard, Los Angeles, CA 90028

Pioneering themed shopping center.

The outdoor shopping center is one of the most ubiquitous architectural features in Los Angeles, and Crossroads of the World was among the first. The complex features a central building designed to resemble an ocean liner surrounded by a small village of cottage-style bungalows, as if the visitor is embarking on a voyage around the world. Though not an immediate success, the concept served as a model for future malls worldwide. In the 1950s, the Crossroads of the World shopping center was converted into an office complex. The Screen Actors Guild; Crosby, Stills, Nash & Young; Jackson Browne; and Alfred Hitchcock all used to rent offices here. In coming years, the area is set for a major redevelopment that will add 950 apartments and a 300-room hotel that will significantly alter Crossroads of the World's quaint atmosphere. Luckily, nearly an exact replica of the central Crossroads building at Disneyworld in Florida is under no threat of redevelopment.

BEST TIME TO GO: Open during business hours.
PARKING: There's free two-hour parking on the adjacent streets, but make sure to read the parking signs.

Angels Flight Railway

350 South Grand Avenue, Los Angeles, CA 90071

Classic public transportation for getting up and down Bunker Hill.

Angels Flight is a cute little funicular railway that has been transporting commuters and tourists 315 feet up downtown's Bunker Hill intermittently since 1901. The original railway ceased operation in 1969 when the area was redeveloped. The whole thing—including the cars, archway and station house—was stored until the railway reconstruction was completed twenty-seven years later. Over the years, the occasional derailment or safety issue has caused the railway to close for a while, but like everything old in Los Angeles, it always eventually comes back.

Angels Flight in its original location on Bunker Hill. *Jack E. Boucher.*

BEST TIME TO GO: After lunch at the Grand Central Market.
PARKING: Meters are your best bet downtown if you can find one. Otherwise, there are a plethora of pay lots in the area.

Watts Towers

1727 East 107th Street, Los Angeles, CA 90002

Folk art masterpiece.

The Watts Towers have the distinction of being one of the only well-known Los Angeles landmarks that aren't an advertisement or commercial building. The Watts Towers were designed and built by Italian immigrant Simon Rodia on his property over a thirty-year period beginning in 1921. Rodia, who had no formal training or specialized equipment, used primarily recycled and found objects in the construction. The towers are built from steel rebar and Rodia's own homemade concrete formula and embedded with broken shards of pottery, glass bottles and other small objects. Look closely and you'll find some new hidden detail every time. Rodia eventually became too old to

The Watts Towers are an example of folk art as well as vernacular architecture. *Adam Papagan.*

continue work on the project and deeded the whole thing to a neighbor. He moved away to live with his sister near Santa Barbara in 1955, never to see his towers again. For years, the city tried to destroy the Watts Towers despite strong opposition from around the world. Engineering tests were ordered in 1959, and the Watts Towers were easily deemed structurally sound. Since then, they have become an official Historic-Cultural Monument and a beloved symbol of the community. The Watts Towers are one of the best examples of folk art and outsider art in California and embody the intrepid creative spirit the state has become famous for.

BEST TIME TO GO: Even when not officially open, the towers are still easily visible from the street.

PARKING: Street parking.

Cedars-Sinai Medical Center

8700 Beverly Boulevard #2900A, Los Angeles, CA 90048

Art-studded hospice for the rich and famous.

Ranked one of the top hospitals in the country, Cedars-Sinai Medical Center has long been the premier destination for celebrities to go to give birth or die. Judy Garland gave birth to Liza Minnelli here in 1946. Pop stars Britney Spears, Christina Aguilera and Madonna have all become new parents here, as have Kourtney Kardashian, Elon Musk, Beyoncé and Jay-Z. Celebrities who spent their last moments on Earth at the hospital include Frank Sinatra, River Phoenix, Johnny Carson, Elizabeth Taylor, Dominique Dunne and Eazy-E. Cedars also possesses an extensive modern and contemporary art collection that is used to decorate the offices, patient rooms and common

Many celebrities receive medical care at Cedars-Sinai Medical Center. *Adam Papagan.*

areas. Most of the work is freely viewable by the public and is the best-kept art secret in LA.

BEST TIME TO GO: Occasionally, the hospital offers guided art tours.
PARKING: It's cheaper to park at the Beverly Center across the street and walk over.

Cinerama Dome

6360 Sunset Boulevard, Los Angeles, CA 90028

LA's second-most famous movie theater.

You can really find anything in Los Angeles, including the only concrete geodesic dome in the world! That dome is the Cinerama Dome, the last vestige of a long-defunct theater chain built to exhibit films in an ultrawide, panoramic format. The theater was built in 1963 to coincide with the premiere of *It's a Mad, Mad, Mad, Mad World*, which was shot in the then new 70mm format. Although other domes were built around the country, the concept never really took off. The Cinerama Dome became a part of the ArcLight Hollywood theater complex in 2002 and was used to show first-run movies and for screening events. The entire ArcLight theater chain closed in 2020, temporarily shuttering the Cinerama Dome, but its landmark status guarantees its future. Despite being decades old, the Cinerama Dome still manages to look futuristic, and thanks to its signature design people will continue to be delighted by it for years to come.

BEST TIME TO GO: Day, but this is a drive-by.
PARKING: It has a parking lot, but since the theater closed, there has been little activity there.

Brown Derby

3377 Wilshire Boulevard, Los Angeles, CA 90010

Former home of hat-shaped restaurant miraculously still standing.

The Brown Derby restaurant and its distinctive bowler hat–shaped building have become synonymous with the Golden Age of Hollywood. The restaurant was actually a chain, with several locations that are often confused with one another. The Hollywood location, located at the famous corner of Hollywood and Vine, was known for its glamorous clientele and for being the birthplace of both the Shirley Temple and the Cobb salad. The Wilshire Boulevard location, frequently depicted in old cartoons, was the only one actually shaped like a hat. When the chain folded in the 1980s, preservationists made arrangements for the iconic dome to be saved. The original Brown Derby hat now sits on top of an otherwise nondescript shopping center in Koreatown called Brown Derby Plaza.

A contemporary view of the original hat-shaped Brown Derby restaurant, now atop a strip mall in Koreatown. *Adam Papagan.*

BEST TIME TO GO: Easiest to see during the day
PARKING: The Brown Derby Plaza has a parking lot.

BRADBURY BUILDING

304 South Broadway, Los Angeles, CA 90013

Architectural anomaly in the heart of downtown.

Although it doesn't look like much from the outside, the building's extraordinary sky-lit atrium of access walkways, stairs and elevators and their ornate ironwork will instantly transport you back to the 1890s. The building was commissioned by Los Angeles gold mining millionaire Lewis L. Bradbury, although he died one year before its completion. The striking design has made the building a popular filming location. Most notably, the Bradbury Building is a setting in the 1982 science fiction film *Blade Runner* as the character J. F. Sebastian's apartment and the climactic rooftop scene. It has been used as an office building for most of the property's history. The LAPD Internal Affairs Department has a fifty-year lease on an office space here.

BEST TIME TO GO: Open daily, but only in the lobby.
PARKING: Limited parking downtown, but there are pay lots and meters.

The Bradbury Building looks ordinary from the outside, but the inside boasts a magnificent atrium. *Jack E. Boucher.*

Beverly Hills City Hall

455 North Rexford Drive, Beverly Hills, CA 90210

The corridor of power in one of America's flashiest cities.

From the very beginning, Beverly Hills has been an ostentatious, image-conscious place. Its opulent, oversized Spanish Revival–style city hall was built in the 1930s during the height of the Great Depression, when the city had fewer than twenty thousand residents. Like many Beverly Hills residents, the city hall has been in a few films, maybe most notably *Beverly Hills Cop*. In addition, it is still the center of most government and civic business.

BEST TIME TO GO: Never crowded. Easily viewable from traffic on Santa Monica Boulevard.

PARKING: The best thing about Beverly Hills is the ample free two-hour street parking found around the city.

Hollywood High School

6000 Santa Monica Boulevard, Los Angeles, CA 90038

Public high school with famous alumni.

One cool thing about Southern California is that practically every high school has a Wikipedia page listing all the famous people who went to school there. When you're from here, getting into show business just doesn't seem that far-fetched. Maybe you know someone in the business already. Maybe you're somebody's kid. Maybe you feel you're just a bit more talented than all the newcomers you see arriving each day. Either way, you're already ahead of a lot of people. Famous alumni of Hollywood High include Carol Burnett, Cher, Judy Garland, John Ritter, Sarah Jessica Parker, Lana Turner and Ricky Nelson. Just think, Hollywood's next big sensation could be handing in their homework right now!

BEST TIME TO GO: Weekends, with fewer kids hanging around. The school itself is closed to the public.

PARKING: It's on Sunset, just off Hollywood, so you'll probably drive by it at some point.

The Stack (Four-Level Interchange)

101/110 Interchange near Downtown Los Angeles

A freeway first.

LA is as famous for its traffic as the weather or anything else. After all, the freeway was invented here. In 1953, that first freeway, the Arroyo Seco Parkway, was joined to the Hollywood Freeway in a four-level interchange, a first-of-its-kind engineering feat. Four directions of traffic cross over one another at the same point. The interchange became a mark of Los Angeles' postwar development boom, appearing on postcards in the 1950s and '60s. Hollywood was quick to take notice, and the Stack, as it came to be known, became a familiar symbol of the hustle and bustle of Los Angeles in the movies. Four-level interchanges have since popped up on freeways around the world, but this was the first. Many traffic-impacted commuters today refer to it as the "Four Letter Interchange."

BEST TIME TO GO: Early Sunday morning when there's no traffic. The best view is getting on the 101 North from the 110 North.
PARKING: Don't park on the freeway.

The Four-Level Interchange is also known as the Stack since four directions of traffic pass atop one another. *Brian Grogan.*

Venice Canals

Entrance at Dell Avenue and 28th Avenue

An Italian-style waterway in the heart of a residential neighborhood.

The original plan for Venice by developer Abbot Kinney was to turn the seaside neighborhood into a simulacra of Venice, Italy, complete with man-made canals and singing gondoliers. The canals were fed by seawater from the ocean a few blocks away, with water running right through the residential lots. The gimmick was initially a hit when it opened in 1905, but by the late 1920s, the novelty had worn off and the city opted to fill in most of the canals to make way for paved roads. One small section of canals managed to escape the steamroller but was left to decay. After a decades-long fight from residents, the canals were finally restored in the early '90s, bringing back the canal water along with curious tourists. Today, it's

Only one residential neighborhood in Venice still retains the original canals. *Carol Highsmith.*

become a very desirable and expensive residential neighborhood; many of the historic homes have been replaced with lot-maximizing megamansions, but the cute little canals remain.

BEST TIME TO GO: On foot, it's beautiful around sunset. By car, anytime will do.
PARKING: I usually just drive through, but if you're on foot, just head over from wherever you parked for Venice Beach.

Beverly Hills Sign

9439 Santa Monica Boulevard, Beverly Hills, CA 90210

SoCal's *other* famous sign.

The Hollywood Sign isn't the only sign you'll want to take a picture with. The Beverly Hills Sign's origins stretch back to 1931, when it was erected as a real estate advertisement, similar to the Hollywood Sign. It's gone away and come back a few times over the years and was never a well-known attraction until the age of social media. That's when it became a major hit, with tourists wanting to prove to their friends back home that they had officially arrived in Beverly Hills. The sign has become so popular that many of the open-air bus companies have altered their routes to incorporate it. The sign is at the end of Rodeo Drive but also sits in the middle of the multi-block Beverly Gardens Park, an art-filled greenbelt that separates the residential and commercial parts of Beverly Hills.

BEST TIME TO GO: Whatever time of day will give you the best light. It's one of the most photographed spots in LA.
PARKING: Lots of free two-hour parking in the surrounding residential neighborhoods.

Self-Realization Fellowship

17190 Sunset Boulevard, Pacific Palisades, CA 90272

Hidden new-age oasis.

A few blocks from the end of Sunset Boulevard in the exclusive beach town of Pacific Palisades is Lake Shrine, operated by the spiritual organization the Self Realization Fellowship. The site's official history is mired in mumbo jumbo, complete with prophetic visions and celebrity name-dropping. Lake Shrine's origins were as a movie studio before being acquired by SRF founder Paramahansa Yogananda in the late 1940s. The Fellowship's grounds boast the aforementioned lake, as well as walking paths, waterfalls, a Dutch windmill and a temple. One of the biggest draws is a thousand-year-old Chinese sarcophagus containing some of Mahatma Gandhi's ashes, apparently the only such site outside of India in the world. The SRF seems to be popular with musicians as well. Elvis was a frequent visitor, and the funerals for George Harrison, Tom Petty and the Cramps' Lux Interior were held here.

BEST TIME TO GO: Advanced reservations are required and book up quickly.
PARKING: Free parking in the lot.

Pacific Design Center

8687 Melrose Avenue, West Hollywood, CA 90069

Eye-catching West Hollywood complex for design.

Driving around West Hollywood, guests often ask, "Hey, what's up with those giant, colorful cubes?" Those cubes are the Pacific Design Center, a 1.5-million-square-foot facility for the design community. The giant complex houses offices, showrooms, galleries and exhibition space for artists and designers but also interior decorators and furniture manufacturers—basically anyone who designs anything. There are galleries that regularly host exhibits, but one of the longest-running events at the PDC is Elton John's annual Oscar party. Other than that, there's not much to see, but at least now you know what they are.

BEST TIME TO GO: Not much to see inside if you're not going to a specific gallery or showroom. It closes at 5:00 p.m.
PARKING: There are surprisingly a lot of meters in this part of West Hollywood. Other than that, it has a lot.

Union Station

800 North Alameda Street, Los Angeles, CA 90012

A grand train station in the car capital of America.

Union Station is considered by many rail fans to be America's last great train station. Union Station was built in the 1930s to consolidate the Union Pacific, Santa Fe and Southern Pacific lines. The station was built on a grand scale incorporating elements of Art Deco, Mission Revival and Streamline Moderne architecture. This makes it a popular backdrop for period films,

Passengers crowd a terminal at Union Station. *Historic American Buildings Survey.*

particularly noir detective stories. Today, it is still a major transportation hub that serves 110,000 travelers and commuters daily. Union Station was also the location of the 2021 Academy Awards ceremony, held during a pandemic year when Hollywood mostly released movies nobody was able to see in theaters.

BEST TIME TO GO: The station is always buzzing, particularly around commute times.

PARKING: There's street parking a little northeast off of Alameda—better yet, take the train!

Chapter 3

PROMINENT PROPERTIES

California embodies our nation's individualist spirit more than any other state. It's always been a place people can come for a fresh start or to try new ideas. It's place where there is an implicit right to decide who you are and how you want to live your life. Naturally, and usually when people get a little too much money, they extend this philosophy to their homes, building ostentatious, over-the-top dwellings. These houses are not typical of how the average person lives but instead offer a glimpse into the zeitgeist of the people who shape the city.

Celebrity Homes

Various locations

The homes of the rich and famous—maybe.

Celebrity homes are some of the most coveted and misunderstood attractions in the LA tourism landscape. The concept of visiting the private residences of the rich and famous is said to have been originated by Bud Delp, the personal driver of Chinese Theater owner Sid Grauman way back in 1935. Basically, as long as there have been movie stars and vehicles large enough to take tourists to their homes, there have been celebrity home tours.

The home of silent film star Harold Lloyd is in Beverly Hills. *Historic American Buildings Survey.*

The truth is that most of the locations visited are not the actual homes of your favorite actor or actress. Locations are passed from tour guide to tour guide during the week or so of training you receive, and precise details get distorted like a game of telephone. As a tour guide, you quickly learn that you can point to virtually any flashy house and say a celebrity lives there, and people will take pictures without really questioning it. The internet has made it easy to do your own research, but it's still hard to know for sure who really lives where. Regardless, it's still nice to spend the afternoon driving around fancy neighborhoods, no matter who lives there. These are private residences; please do not disturb occupants.

BEST TIME TO GO: Best visibility in the daytime.
PARKING: Many of the streets in the nicer parts of town do not allow street parking at any time, so be quick if you jump out to get a picture.

GREYSTONE MANSION

905 Loma Vista Drive, Beverly Hills, CA 90210

One of Beverly Hills' oldest mansions and open to the public.

The sprawling Greystone Mansion was once the most expensive home in California. The mansion was built by oil tycoon Edward Doheny as a gift for his son Ned and his family. On February 16, 1929, four months after Ned and his wife, Lucy, along with their five children, moved into Greystone, Doheny died in a guest bedroom in a murder-suicide with his secretary, Hugh Plunkett. Circumstances are debated, but Lucy remarried and lived in the house until 1955, when she sold off much of the property. With the remainder under threat of demolition, the City of Beverly Hills purchased Greystone in 1965 and turned it into a public park. Greystone's grandeur has made it a natural film location, appearing in *X-Men*, *There Will Be Blood* and *The Big Lebowski*. The vibe is a little stuffy, but if you want to see a mansion up close *and* a site for film and TV locations, it's a double whammy.

BEST TIME TO GO: Morning.
PARKING: Free.

The impressive Greystone Mansion is today a city park with its grounds open to the public. *Historic American Buildings Survey.*

Huntington Library

1151 Oxford Road, San Marino, CA 91108

Sprawling gardens and research library stuffed with art.

The Huntington is one of Los Angeles' most impressive estates turned museums. Henry Huntington was a land baron and railroad magnate who played a major role in the development of Southern California. He made his money working for his uncle Collis, who owned one of the four major railroads in the United States at the time. This set Henry up to be able to purchase and develop large tracts of the newly forming California. When Collis died, Henry swiftly married his uncle's widow (a fact proudly stated in the museum's brochure), and the two combined their fortunes to amass one of the largest private collections of European and American art in the world. They also built a massive compound to store it in and live out their final days. The collection was opened to the public after the Huntingtons' deaths in the late '20s. The Huntington features a research library containing historic manuscripts and correspondences, the original house packed to the ceiling with antiques, several designated art galleries, a greenhouse, Hellenic sculptures and acres of lush international botanical gardens. The grounds are massive, and you could easily spend a day or two exploring everything. It's a popular attraction crowded with people and plants from around the world, a reflection of the Southern California that the Huntingtons helped found.

BEST TIME TO GO: The grounds are huge, and you have to do a lot of walking so go in the winter or spring, not when it's hot. Advance reservations are required, and the museum frequently sells out.

PARKING: There's a free parking lot, but they frequently sell more tickets than parking spaces, so you may have to park in the surrounding neighborhood and walk in.

Gamble House

4 Westmoreland Place, Pasadena, CA 91103

Excessive yet tasteful Craftsman mansion.

Of all the mansions you can tour around town, the Gamble House is easily the most tasteful. The Gamble family, having amassed tremendous wealth as

The influential Gamble House may be more recognizable as a filming location for *Back to the Future*. *Carol Highsmith.*

part of the Proctor & Gamble empire, commissioned the house in 1908 as a winter residence. However, the credit for the Craftsman-style home's beauty should go to the brother-brother architectural team Greene and Greene, which pioneered the Arts and Crafts design movement. Every aspect of the house, from the materials to the layout to the furniture, was meticulously planned, with common themes and motifs flowing freely between designs. Everywhere you turn, there is a new small detail to appreciate. The house offers several variations of its tour, but the standard docent-led tour is more than sufficient. And yes, this was also Doc Brown's house in *Back to the Future*.

BEST TIME TO GO: First thing in the morning during the summer. These old houses don't have air conditioning. At other times of the year, it's a lot more manageable.

PARKING: Free street parking in front of the museum.

Ennis House

2607 Glendower Avenue, Los Angeles, CA 90027

Imposing temple-like home and filming location.

The Mayan-inspired, Frank Lloyd Wright–designed Ennis House is one of the most striking homes in Los Angeles. The house is constructed from thousands of precast concrete blocks that, over the years, have cracked and crumbled, resulting in the need for constant renovation. The Ennis house's unique look has featured prominently in many productions, including *Day of the Locust*, *Blade Runner*, *Rush Hour*, *Westworld* and even *Curb Your Enthusiasm*. The façade is also used as the home in *The House on Haunted Hill*, despite the interior sets clearly depicting a Victorian design. When the house sold to a private buyer in 2011, a condition of the sale was an easement that allows for public viewing at least twelve days a year, with the condition being extended to subsequent buyers. In practice, however, this clause is rarely honored or enforced, so getting up-close access to the house can be difficult. The more visitor-friendly, Wright-designed Hollyhock House is located down the street. Private residence; please do not disturb occupants.

BEST TIME TO GO: Easiest to see during the day but also creepy at night.
PARKING: Easy parking right out front.

Virginia Robinson Gardens

1008 Elden Way, Beverly Hills, CA 90210

Lush botanical gardens located on one of Beverly Hill's original estates.

Virginia Robinson was the first "First Lady of Beverly Hills." Virginia and her husband, Harry (founder of Robinson's department stores), were able to snatch up several acres of Beverly Hills real estate around the time of the city's founding and established the area's first estate in 1911. Their two-bedroom home would be considered small by today's standards but was quite lavish for the time. A guest book displayed in the front room features the signatures of Jimmy Stewart and the many other celebrities and socialites the Robinsons regularly entertained. The jewel of the property is the lush botanical gardens, cared for by an army of landscapers and horticulturalists. Virginia lived to the ripe old age of one hundred and, before she died, deeded the house and the gardens to the County of Los Angeles. Since then, the grounds have been open on a limited basis for docent-led tours. They're still peaceful and classy, a far cry from the "Real Housewives" that people associate Beverly Hills with today.

BEST TIME TO GO: Advanced reservations are required and tend to sell out. I took the morning tour to avoid the heat.
PARKING: Free parking on the grounds.

The Virginia Robinson Gardens is one of the original and most intact Beverly Hills estates. *Adam Papagan.*

Stahl House

1635 Woods Drive, West Hollywood, CA 90069

Frequently photographed modernist home with sweeping views.

Even if you're not a huge devotee of modern architecture, you've probably seen the Stahl House in a movie, TV show or ad campaign. Similar to the Eames House, the Space Age bachelor pad, with its sleek glass frame and overhanging steel roof, was built as part of *Architectural Digest*'s Case Study House program, which challenged designers to build aesthetically stylish but inexpensive modern homes from readily available industrial materials. The Stahls were not international jet setters but a middle-class family from the South Bay, back when a middle-class family with a single income could afford a cliffside home in Los Angeles. Construction on the house, partially paid for by sponsorships from *Architectural Digest*, began in 1959, and soon a modernist icon was born. Today, the home is no longer a private residence but has instead been opened up to the paying public. The home's panoramic views of most of LA's major landmarks really are breathtaking. During the tour, you are allowed to sit on modern furniture where you can gaze through the floor-to-ceiling windows at the city below and pretend you're in an episode of *Mad Men*.

BEST TIME TO GO: They say the twilight tour is the best, but it books up months in advance.

PARKING: They direct you where to park when you get there, but if you're one of the first two cars to arrive, you get to park in the carport as if you live there.

Eames House

203 Chautauqua Boulevard, Pacific Palisades, CA 90272

Home and studio of the iconic chair-designing couple.

The Eames House was both an experimental architectural project and the personal residence and studio of landmark husband-and-wife design team Charles and Ray Eames. This unique home was built as part of *Architectural Digest*'s Case Study House initiative, which challenged designers to build stylish but economical modern homes from readily available industrial materials. Of the twenty-five Case Study homes built, the Eames House is considered the pinnacle. The inside seems lived in but also well curated. Modern yet cozy, just like the couple themselves. Today, the house is a museum operated by the Eames Foundation and is a pilgrimage site for fans of modern design.

The home of Charles and Ray Eames was designed by the couple themselves. *Carol Highsmith.*

BEST TIME TO GO: Reservations required.
PARKING: Free parking at the end of the road.

THE CHEMOSPHERE

7776 Toreyson Drive, Los Angeles, CA

Quintessential Space Age domicile.

Built by famed modernist architect John Lautner, the Chemosphere looks like something straight out of *The Jetsons*. Lautner came up with the UFO-like design as a solution for fitting the house on its narrow hillside lot. The home juts out from the hillside and is accessible only by funicular. Because of its Space Age design, the house has been used in productions like *The Outer Limits* and parodied on *The Simpsons* (as the home of washed-up actor Troy McClure). The house is currently owned by the Taschen family, who make those giant, arty coffee table books. As a special bonus, there is also a prefabricated, spaceship-inspired Futura house at the base of the property.

BEST TIME TO GO: Around sunset.
PARKING: Very little street parking on narrow streets.

O'Neill House

507 North Rodeo Drive, Beverly Hills, CA 90210

Playfully designed mansion at the end of Rodeo Drive.

The O'Neill House, also called the Little Mermaid House and the Birthday Cake House, was designed to look like a surreal creation by the Spanish architect Antoni Gaudí. The home, owned by art dealers Don and Sandy O'Neill, started life as a typical two-story Beverly Hills mansion. In the '70s, the couple began an ambitious Art Nouveau–style remodel of their home. They began with the back guest house and, through the years, expanded to the front of the house and the interior, adding a swirling roof and oval-shaped rooms. Don passed away before the project was completed, but it is believed that Sandy still owns the property today. Private residence; please do not disturb occupants.

BEST TIME TO GO: Get out of the car and walk around to the back alley; it's even more ornate.
PARKING: Street parking.

The guest quarters of the O'Neill House were the first to be built in this whimsical style. *Carol Highsmith.*

Spelling Manor

594 South Mapelton Drive, Los Angeles, CA 90024

LA's largest house, but not on purpose.

Melrose Place, *The Love Boat*, *Beverly Hills, 90210*—Aaron Spelling was known for producing some of the biggest shows in television history. He also used his massive fortune to produce the biggest and most over-the-top house in Los Angeles' history. The 56,500-square-foot chateau-style mansion has an incredible fourteen bedrooms, twenty-seven bathrooms, a gift-wrapping room, an entire floor of closets, a gym, a room for housewife Candy Spelling's doll collection and parking for one hundred cars. The Spellings began construction on their gargantuan estate in the late 1980s. The original plans didn't call for the house to be so grandiose, but Candy, who was very hands-on during the design process, misread the blueprints and kept insisting everything be made bigger. Every room in the house ended up being twice the scale they needed to be. After Aaron's death, the house sold for $85 million in 2011, the most expensive real estate sale in the United States at the time. The Manor sold most recently in 2019 for $119.7 million, again another record. Private residence; please do not disturb occupants.

BEST TIME TO GO: Not much to see. This is a drive-by if you're in the area.
PARKING: Easy parking around the adjacent Holmby Park.

Frederick R. Weisman Art Foundation

265 North Carolwood Drive, Los Angeles, CA 90077

Home turned museum of art collecting mogul.

Businessman Frederick R. Weisman made *beaucoup* bucks as founder of one of the first Toyota distributors in North America. He and his wife, Marica Simon (sister of art collector Norton Simon), spent much of their fortune collecting works by Warhol, Rothko, Lichtenstein, Picasso, Harring and other leading modern and contemporary artists of their day. They used it to decorate every available inch of wall space in their Holmby Hills estate. When they divorced, they divided up the collection. Marica donated her half to Cedars-Sinai Hospital, while Fred planned to display his half in his own museum. When plans never materialized, he had the idea of converting his own home into a museum open to the public at select times. Weisman passed away in 1994, but the foundation is still going strong. The collection really is impressive and allows the average person to experience what it's like living in a home surrounded by tens of millions of dollars' worth of art.

BEST TIME TO GO: Visitation is by appointment only, but they're easy to get.
PARKING: Docent will direct you where to park.

Chapter 4

MUSEUMS

Contrary to what some snobs may tell you, Los Angeles is not devoid of culture. In fact, we continue to be a leading voice in shaping culture worldwide. After all, the internet was partially developed at UCLA in 1969. We're also the birthplace of the Walt Disney Company, currently one of the world's most powerful cultural conglomerates. Los Angeles is also home to a very vibrant museum scene. The concentration of wealth here means that many are exceedingly well funded and feature world-class examples of fine art. There's also a lot of quirky museums that can leave you befuddled as to why they even exist in the first place. If nothing else, many are also a great source of air conditioning on a hot day.

Natural History Museum of Los Angeles County

900 West Exposition Boulevard, Los Angeles, CA 90007

Exhibition hall for very old things and perennial school field trip favorite.

Most major cities have a natural history museum, and they're all sort of the same but a little different. This is true of the Natural History Museum of Los Angeles County, which is the largest institution of its kind on the West Coast. The three-story museum houses 35 million specimens, which cover a whopping 4.5 billion years of history. There's an entire wing dedicated to dinosaur fossils, and its collection of mineralogy is dazzling.

The Natural History Museum features multiple halls of lifelike dioramas. *Adam Papagan.*

One of the popular exhibits is the vast collection of taxidermized creatures displayed in extensively detailed dioramas of their natural habitat. Even though these animals have been dead and stuffed for decades, they appear eerily lifelike. It feels as if they could hop out of their enclosures and mosey into the gift shop at any moment. The Natural History Museum has had mostly the same stuff there since I was a kid, which is another thing people really like about it.

BEST TIME TO GO: Weekdays if you can swing it. The weekends are more crowded. Try to catch the butterfly pavilion in the spring or summer.
PARKING: Pay lot or street parking in the neighborhood south of Exposition Park.

Los Angeles County Arboretum

301 North Baldwin Avenue, Arcadia, CA 91007

County-sponsored place for plants.

The Los Angeles County Arboretum features plant species from across the world. *Adam Papagan.*

Located east of Downtown LA in the suburb of Arcadia, the Los Angeles County Arboretum is a historical site and garden containing plant species from around the world. Although the area has been inhabited since pre-Columbian times, businessman Elias "Lucky" Baldwin developed most of the surrounding neighborhood in the late 1800s. Baldwin built an elaborate Queen Anne–style cottage on the property and imported several peafowl whose descendants still roam the gardens. Like many beautiful California locations, it has been featured in many film and TV productions, most notably in the opening sequence of *Fantasy Island*. The Arboretum is a little off the beaten path but is a nice break if you're looking to get away from LA's celebrity-centric attractions. The peacocks freely roaming the grounds are an added visual treat.

BEST TIME TO GO: Late morning before it gets too hot.
PARKING: It has a free lot.

Los Angeles Zoo

5333 Zoo Drive, Los Angeles, CA 90027

Municipal zoo with frequent escape attempts.

Zoos are kind of sad in general, but the Los Angeles Zoo holds its own sort of charm and personal nostalgia for locals who grew up here. The zoo itself is typical for a midsize zoo, with chimpanzees, elephants, gorillas, giraffes and more, but it also has one of the only mountain tapirs on display worldwide. It's also led a successful breeding program to save the nearly extinct California condor. The favorite thing for many here is the carousel, where instead of horses, guests ride on figures shaped like different animals. This might be your only chance to ride a panda. The zoo has been the location of more than thirty-five animal escape attempts, including a gorilla named Evelyn, who was able to roam the zoo for more than an hour before being recaptured. The zoo is wholly owned and operated by the City of Los Angeles, which may explain the breakouts.

BEST TIME TO GO: Many animals are most active in the morning.
PARKING: Miraculously, the zoo still has free parking.

Mount Wilson Observatory

Follow Angeles Crest Highway all the way to the top.

The best place in Southern California to see the stars.

Hollywood may be the place to see movie stars, but if you want to see some actual stars, head up to the Mount Wilson Observatory. The observatory was founded with a grant from the Carnegie Institution in 1904 and, for a time, contained some of the largest telescopes in the world. These telescopes have made many groundbreaking discoveries, including the revelation that the universe extends beyond the Milky Way. The drive into the mountains is beautiful as well and can make you forget you're less than an hour from Downtown Los Angeles. This one is out of the way (and out of cellphone range) from Los Angeles but is well worth the trek for cosmic enthusiasts.

BEST TIME TO GO: The views are beautiful during the day, but try to get access to one of the special night events where you can look through the telescope.
PARKING: Parking lot.

Griffith Observatory

2800 East Observatory Road, Los Angeles, CA 90027

Art Deco observatory bringing astronomy to the people.

The Griffith Observatory has been a beloved LA landmark since its opening in 1935. The observatory was built at the bequest of Griffith J. Griffith, who wanted to bring astronomy to the masses. While most research observatories are located on far-off mountaintops away from light pollution, Griffith Observatory is instead an educational institution located in the heart of the city. The view of the Hollywood Sign and free admission have made it a

The Griffith Observatory allows public viewings through its telescope. *Library of Congress.*

popular destination for tourists. The observatory figures prominently in the plot of *Rebel Without a Cause*, and a bust of James Dean can be found on the west edge of the overlook.

BEST TIME TO GO: At night, they let you look through the telescope.
PARKING: Parking used to be free here, but now it can cost up to fifteen dollars per hour. Basically, the parking spots make minimum wage.

California Science Center

700 Exposition Park Drive, Los Angeles, CA 90037

Interactive, kid-friendly learning space.

Where else can you find ancient treasures plundered from the tomb of Tutankhamun and a vehicle that's traveled back and forth from outer space at the same institution? The California Science Center is a massive complex of science exhibits relating to everything from ecosystems to aerodynamics. It's one of those "makes learning fun" types of museums, so there are interactive exhibits and buttons to push all over the place. The centerpiece of the museum's collection is the Space Shuttle Endeavor, whose orbiters were originally constructed in California. General admission to the museum is free, but the IMAX and special traveling exhibitions like King Tut and Bodies cost extra. Since this is a free attraction, it can get very crowded, particularly on the weekends.

BEST TIME TO GO: Late afternoons on weekdays. It's a popular field trip spot, so on weekday mornings, the museum is filled with excited kids.
PARKING: Pay lot or street parking in the neighborhood south of Exposition Park.

The Autry Museum of the American West

Griffith Park, 4700 Western Heritage Way, Los Angeles, CA 90027

Cowboy museum offering a truer picture of the Old West.

Los Angeles is the end of the Old West. In fact, if you went any farther west, you'd literally fall right off the continent. Hollywood did a lot to inject the mythic image of the West into popular culture. Actors like John Wayne came to embody the supposed American ideals of grit and responsibility while presenting a romanticized, but inaccurate, depiction of the frontier. The Autry Museum of the American West, named for singing cowboy and businessman Gene Autry, however, is a lot more than saddles and western movie costumes. The museum is dedicated to exploring an inclusive history of the American West from a holistic perspective. Here, you can find thousands of statues, paintings, textiles, firearms, musical instruments and other objects in ever-changing rotating exhibits that inspire new interpretations of the West. The museum presents contemporary and historical exhibitions, year-round programs for children, intellectual forums and the Native Voices at the Autry performing arts series.

BEST TIME TO GO: Weekdays. It closes early, so check the hours before going.
PARKING: Free.

California African American Museum

600 State Drive, Los Angeles, CA 90037

Free museum with holistic approach to its subject matter.

The California African American Museum flies under the radar, but it's free and definitely worth checking out. Established in 1981, its mission statement is "to research, collect, preserve, and interpret for public enrichment the history, art, and culture of African Americans with an emphasis on California and the western United States." There are three main galleries, so there's a good amount of stuff here, but it's not overwhelming. On a given visit, you're likely to see fine art, installations, multimedia and historic artifacts, so it's a nice mixture. Located in Exposition Park, CAAM is easy to squeeze in after visiting the Natural History Museum or California Science Center.

BEST TIME TO GO: Hardly crowded, especially on a weekday.
PARKING: Pay lot or street parking in the neighborhood south of Exposition Park.

Martial Arts History Museum

201 N Brand Avenue Suite B100, Glendale, CA 91203

Beautiful Downtown Glendale's very own karate museum.

There's something so intriguing about a museum dedicated to one very specific thing. Seeing room after room dedicated to an obscure subject or collection can really help you appreciate something you may never have thought twice about but is clearly the curator's life's work. Glendale's Martial Arts History Museum is dedicated to the art, history and practice of martial arts and how they have become intertwined with American culture. There are sections devoted to martial arts from different regions across the world, as well as exhibits on anime and the media. There are also some fun artifacts and props, including Ralph Macchio's actual headband from *The Karate Kid* and the infamous gopher chucks from *Kung Pow! Enter the Fist*. My mark of a good museum is if you leave having learned something, and this museum really makes you realize the impact martial arts have had on popular culture.

BEST TIME TO GO: Closed Mondays and Tuesdays.
PARKING: Street parking.

Museum of Jurassic Technology

9341 Venice Boulevard, Culver City, CA 90232

A pair of possibly the world's most esoteric museums.

The Museum of Jurassic Technology is tough to explain. Essentially, it's a museum about questioning the concept of museums. The enigmatic museum was founded by David and Diana Wilson, who received a MacArthur "genius grant" for their work. The bewildering, multilevel layout is filled with unique exhibits about engineering, science, art and natural history, all cryptic in nature. Display cases are left intentionally empty, and the explanation of artifacts is deliberately dense and confusing. Some of the exhibits are real, and some are completely made up. The museum plays up the ambiguity, and it's left up to the visitor to interpret. Part cabinet of curiosities, part art installation, part prank, the Museum of Jurassic Technology is a trippy and unique way to spend an afternoon. Make sure to visit the equally eccentric

Center for Land Use Interpretation next door, which examines the banality of built environments in illuminating and excruciating detail.

BEST TIME TO GO: Open afternoons and evenings Thursday through Sunday.
PARKING: Street parking.

The Bhagavad-gita Museum

3764 Watseka Avenue, Los Angeles, CA 90034

Trippy Hare Krishna compound.

This is an odd one but totally worth checking out if you have the time. The Bhagavad-gita Museum is a set of eleven dioramas depicting the teachings of the Hare Krishna movement. Opened in 1977, the museum featured, at the time, state-of-the-art sound and light displays. The show controls have been updated a few times, but the dioramas still possess their retro psychedelic charm. After visiting the museum, you can pop over to the bland but hearty on-site health food restaurant for lunch. This is one is not recommended if you're the kind of person who is easily talked into things, as rumors that the International Society for Krishna Consciousness is, in fact, a cult have swirled for years.

BEST TIME TO GO: Call to verify hours.
PARKING: Street parking.

Museum of Neon Art

216 South Brand Boulevard, Glendale, CA 91204

Lighted signs recontextualized as art.

A neon sign honoring Route 66, not far from the Museum of Neon Art. *Carol Highsmith.*

Who can resist the alluring call of a bright neon sign? Outside of Las Vegas, Los Angeles is one of the best places to see lighted signs in North America. Most of these signs advertise businesses, and when these businesses close, their colorful neon signs are often destined for the junkyard. Luckily, Glendale's Museum of

Neon Art has been there to step in to save and exhibit these beloved buzzing signs. The small but efficient museum is the final resting place for the signage of many beloved Los Angeles institutions, including the Brown Derby and the Earl Carroll Theater. Being able to observe the pieces at eye level adds new levels of appreciation for the artistry that went into them. Although the signs are the main draw, the museum also exhibits other forms of electric art and offers classes for beginners trying to keep the neon tradition alive.

BEST TIME TO GO: Occasionally, during warmer months, the museum hosts "cruises" around the city to see still active signs in person.
PARKING: Street parking and also many public lots (some free) around Glendale.

Los Angeles County Museum of Art (LACMA)

5905 Wilshire Boulevard, Los Angeles, CA 90036

Multifaceted museum with a collection from around the globe.

The centerpiece of Museum Row, the Los Angeles County Museum of Art is the largest art museum in the western United States. The complex of architecturally mismatched buildings houses more than 120,000 objects spanning the totality of art history. Many of the special exhibitions focus on contemporary and modern art, but my favorite pieces are the ones dating back to ancient times. The museum features entire wings dedicated to Latin

One of the most well-known pieces in LACMA's collection is *Urban Light. Carol Highsmith.*

American, Asian, classical and Islamic art. The institution's high profile has made it a fundraising juggernaut, with an endowment believed to exceed $100 million. This has allowed it to acquire and commission many large-scale works, including Chris Burden's exceedingly photographed *Urban Light*, a collection of 202 vintage streetlights arranged into a grid at the front of the museum.

BEST TIME TO GO: Weekdays are your best bet. It can get really crowded on the weekends.
PARKING: There's a lot, but you can usually find a meter or even free parking on 6th Street.

The Broad

221 South Grand Avenue, Los Angeles, CA 90012

Contemporary art museum seen prominently on social media.

Since opening in 2015, the Broad Contemporary Art Museum has quickly become one of the most Instagrammable museums in LA. The museum was founded by billionaires Eli and Edythe Broad to house their personal art collection, funded by a mixture of public and private money. The museum features major works from artists like Jeff Koons, Andy Warhol, Ed Ruscha and Cindy Sherman, as well as Yayoi Kusama's famous *Infinity Mirrored Room* installation. You've definitely seen it on social media—probably a lot. The Broads are some of the biggest philanthropists and art patrons in Los Angeles. My theory is that Eli made his fortune building ugly, oversized McMansions, and these free museums are a means to soothe his guilty conscience for developing over so much of California's natural beauty.

BEST TIME TO GO: Open daily.
PARKING: It's really hard to park in that part of downtown, so your best bet is in the lot.

The Getty

1200 Getty Center Drive, Los Angeles, CA 90049

Sprawling museum complex with mountain views.

The Getty Center is in a sprawling mountain-top compound. *Carol Highsmith.*

The Getty Center can be overwhelming. The size of the collection is impressive and staggering, but the layout of the galleries can be a lot for even seasoned museum hounds. It's rare that I've been here and seen anyone having a really great time. Even so, the grounds and garden are beautiful, and the hillside provides one of the best views anywhere in West LA. The original museum, the Getty Villa, located in the Pacific Palisades, focuses on ancient Greek and Roman art and is easier to knock out in half a day. Occasionally, the museum will get in hot water for having known fakes or possessing stolen antiquities and will have to hand them over to their countries of origin. J. Paul Getty, the museum's namesake, has somewhat of a mixed reputation as well, famously refusing to pay the ransom for his grandson after he was kidnaped.

BEST TIME TO GO: Toward the end of the day to catch the sunset. You'll be exhausted after.

PARKING: Local residents have ensured that there is no free parking anywhere, so you have to pay to park at the museum.

Norton Simon Museum

411 West Colorado Boulevard, Pasadena, CA 91105

Classy and concise gallery for fine arts.

My pick for the best art museum in Los Angeles is not the Getty or LACMA but rather the Norton Simon Museum in Pasadena. This slightly out-of-the-way museum is home to thousands of artworks, primarily from Asia and Europe, as well as an expansive sculpture garden. The museum was once known as the Pasadena Art Museum and, at one time, was the only major art museum in California between La Jolla and San Francisco. After a string of financial missteps, industrialist Norton Simon stepped in to finance the museum, essentially to display his own collection. The curation today is still based on this original collection, and on any given visit, you're likely to see Van Goghs, Raphaels and other works you've seen in your art history textbook. Although it's not as much bang for your buck as the Getty, the Norton Simon's size is much more manageable.

BEST TIME TO GO: Open Thursday to Monday.
PARKING: Parking lot.

Pasadena's Norton Simon Museum is better curated and less crowded than some similar institutions in the area. *Carol Highsmith.*

Hammer Museum

10899 Wilshire Boulevard, Los Angeles, CA 90024

A more contemporary contemporary art museum curated by UCLA.

If you're into art museums and looking for something a little hipper than the Getty or LACMA, the Hammer just may be your spot. The museum was opened in 1990 to house the personal art collection of industrialist

Armand Hammer but has since fallen under the operation of the University of California–Los Angeles. The museum has multiple galleries with exhibitions that rotate every few months. The focus here is on contemporary art, often with an emphasis on artists or groups typically left out of mainstream art institutions. They also have the Billy Wilder Theater, which frequently hosts screenings, often preceded by an introduction from the faculty of UCLA's Film and Television program. Admission to the museum and most events is free, but some events cost extra.

BEST TIME TO GO: Closed Mondays.
PARKING: There's an underground lot. A few blocks away, there's also free two-hour parking at the lot on Broxton.

Craft Contemporary

5814 Wilshire Boulevard, Los Angeles, CA 90036

Unique museum featuring underseen creative works.

Here's something Mom might like. Originally named the Craft and Folk Art Museum, the Craft Contemporary is the only institution on the West Coast of the United States to focus exclusively on crafts. The museum is a non-collecting institution, so exhibitions change frequently. Because of the museum's emphasis on artists not represented by large art institutions, you're guaranteed to see innovative and creative work here you've not seen before. Past exhibitions have included large-scale dioramas, abstract woven tapestries and a room where everything was covered in shag carpeting. The unique exhibits provide a great aesthetic counterbalance to the prehistoric fossils of the La Brea Tar Pits and supercars of the Peterson Auto Museum, also found on Museum Row.

BEST TIME TO GO: Closed Monday and Tuesday.
PARKING: Pay lots across the street at LACMA and the Tar Pits. You might also get lucky with street parking.

Museum of Contemporary Art (MOCA)

250 South Grand Avenue, Los Angeles, CA 90012

Underutilized space for contemporary art.

MOCA has cool stuff, but for whatever reason it's not nearly as beloved as other area museums. The museum's focus is mostly on European and American art created since 1940. It seems to specialize in large-scale and installation pieces that take up entire rooms of the galleries. The majority of the museum's permanent collection comes from donations from a handful of very prominent donors, so a lot of the work can seem repetitive. Yes, the bulk of the collection was created by white men, but apparently, the museum's curation staff is working on it. The best part of MOCA may be its gift shop, which carries many unique functional and decorative items and is my go-to for last-minute Christmas shopping. MOCA also operates the nearby Geffen Contemporary in Little Tokyo, which is less formal and exhibits more experimental works. A recent donation has allowed both locations to waive admission fees for all.

BEST TIME TO GO: Weekday mornings. Reservations are required, but you can make them when you get there.

PARKING: There's a lot. Sometimes you can find a meter near the Music Center.

Murals

Around the city, but high concentrations around Hollywood

Art around town.

Some of the most interesting art in the city can be found on the sides of buildings and the walls of back alleys. Nearly every neighborhood in Los Angeles is filled with colorful murals depicting celebrities, local heroes and days gone by—you will barely go a block without finding a Kobe Bryant mural. The temporary nature of the murals means that they can go up or disappear overnight, but here are a few of my favorites that have had a surprising longevity:

> *You Are a Star* (1665 Wilcox Avenue, Los Angeles, CA 90028): This delightfully amateurish mural depicts a cavalcade of Hollywood legends

Hollywood's *You Are a Star* mural was literally defaced before later being restored. *Adam Papagan.*

in a packed movie theater facing forward as if the viewer were the one up on the big screen. Some stars, like Marlon Brando, are easy to pick out, while others have faded to become hardly recognizable, but it's still fun trying to figure out who everyone is supposed to be.

Jim Morrison (15 Paloma Avenue, Venice, CA 90291): The Doors are one of the best bands to ever come out of Los Angeles. The group had its roots in Venice Beach, so fittingly, a shirtless, three-story-tall Jim Morrison towers over an alley just off the boardwalk.

Harbor Freeway Overture (just east of the 110 Freeway in downtown): This mural by artist Kent Twitchell is a local favorite. This photorealistic image of the Los Angeles Chamber Orchestra members is instantly recognizable to commuters along the 110. The mural has stood for decades, meaning more people have probably seen it than the actual orchestra.

The mural of the Los Angeles Chamber Orchestra is viewed daily by thousands of commuters along the Harbor Freeway. *Adam Papagan.*

The Great Wall of Los Angeles (12900 Oxnard Street, North Hollywood, CA 91606): This enormous mural, designed by artist Judith Baca and completed by a team of more than four hundred volunteers, shows the history of California from the perspective of women and minorities. The mural's many panels depict Native American history as well as tributes to the LGBTQIA community and the ongoing struggle for civil rights. With so many of the city's murals paying homage to celebrities, the Great Wall of Los Angeles provides a more complete window into LA's real history.

BEST TIME TO GO: Follow the natural light.
PARKING: Varies.

The Academy Museum of Motion Pictures

6067 Wilshire Boulevard, Los Angeles, CA 90036

Carefully curated museum dedicated to promoting the film industry.

One of LA's newest high-profile attractions is the Academy Museum of Motion Pictures. After many delays and much anticipation, the museum finally opened in 2021 and is dedicated to the film industry's history, science and cultural impact. That roughly translates to movie props, screenplays and tons of Oscar statues. You'll see old friends like E.T., C-3PO and the shark from *Jaws*. The coolest feature is probably the Dolby-sponsored glass-domed terrace at the top of the museum and its view of the surrounding area. Many of the exhibits are awkwardly geared toward making Hollywood appear much more inclusive than it has been, but there's serious potential here. The Academy Museum is in the same vicinity as LACMA, the La Brea Tar Pits, the Petersen Automotive Museum and the Craft Contemporary, so it's easy to make a museum day of it.

BEST TIME TO GO: The museum can get crowded, so weekday mornings are your best bet if you can swing it.

PARKING: The museum has self-parking and valet (hey, it's Hollywood!), but you can probably snag a meter on 6th Street.

The Academy Museum in its original iteration as the May Company department store. *Historic American Buildings Survey.*

Hollywood Museum

1660 North Highland Avenue, Hollywood, CA 90028

Show business museum brimming with pop culture heirlooms.

Although it's walking distance from Ripley's, a selfie museum and two wax museums, the Hollywood Museum is lightyears better than any of the other museums on Hollywood Boulevard. The museum is home to an extensive collection of props, costumes, photographs and other entertainment memorabilia laid out across four floors. Some of the exhibitions are a bit disorganized, but it's a thrill to come face to face with Pee-wee's bicycle, the Maltese Falcon and other beloved pop culture artifacts. The Hollywood Museum is housed in the old Max Factor Building, named for the pioneering beautician and make-up artist. Factor's original make-up rooms, each themed around a different hair color, are re-created on the first floor. Factor is credited for gifting many actresses with their signature look, including turning Lucille Ball into a redhead. A favorite touch, however, is the museum's clean, impeccably restored vintage bathrooms.

The Hollywood Museum features a beautifully restored vintage restroom. *Adam Papagan.*

BEST TIME TO GO: Never that crowded.
PARKING: Two-hour parking around Selma before 6:00 p.m.

Grammy Museum

800 West Olympic Boulevard, Los Angeles, CA 90015

Music history as told by the recording industry.

Even if you don't like the Grammys, the Grammy Museum is pretty cool. The museum opened in 2008 and is in a similar vein to other music museums like the Rock & Roll Hall of Fame and Seattle's Museum of Pop

Culture. You'll find instruments, wardrobes and other artifacts but also interactive exhibits focused on the recording process. It also has regularly changing special exhibitions. It's a validating experience for fans, seeing their favorite artists presented in a respectable museum format. The Ramones exhibit even featured an unaffiliated, volunteer Joey Ramone impersonator. The museum regularly holds performances and artist conversations, which routinely sell out, so check its calendar.

BEST TIME TO GO: It's crowded for events, but weekdays are pretty chilled out. Closed Tuesdays.
PARKING: There's parking off Olympic west of the 110 freeway. Otherwise, there's a parking structure.

Museum of Flying

3100 Airport Avenue, Santa Monica, CA 90405

Kid-approved site for airplane history.

Southern California has a rich history as the one-time center of aviation manufacturing in the United States. Santa Monica's Museum of Flying honors this history, as well as that of the Douglas Aircraft Company, formerly headquartered in Santa Monica. The small but informative museum features more than a dozen vintage and historic aircraft, as well as a replica of the Wright brothers' plane used in the movie *A Night at the Museum*. There's also an actual cockpit for a FedEx plane they let you climb around in and flip the knobs.

BEST TIME TO GO: Hardly ever crowded. Closes at 4:00 p.m.
PARKING: Parking lot.

Travel Town Museum

5200 Zoo Drive, Los Angeles, CA 90027

Experience the railroads of LA's past.

Every family has at least one rail fan. Usually it's a wide-eyed child or cranky old man. I personally fall somewhere in the middle, but if you have at least a passing interest in trains, Travel Town is a nice stop. The railroad museum opened in 1952 with the mission of preserving and displaying locomotives, which were being swiftly decommissioned at the time. The outdoor museum features dozens of engines, coaches and artifacts related to train travel. The trains are in various states of restoration, but many are open and exploration is encouraged. There's also a miniature railroad that takes you on a loop around the grounds. It's a simple little museum and a pleasant window into a simpler past.

BEST TIME TO GO: This is a midday kind of place.
PARKING: Free parking in the lot.

Petersen Automotive Museum

6060 Wilshire Boulevard, Los Angeles, CA 90036

A temple for Los Angeles' automobile obsession.

All of Los Angeles is kind of like a car museum. The culture, the amount of time we spend in our vehicles and the large number of affluent residents means that seeing a vintage low rider or street-legal race car rolling down your block isn't all that strange. Within this autopian paradise, we find the Petersen Automotive Museum, one of the largest institutions of its kind in the world. It has classic cars, concept cars, supercars, motorcycles and even a few famous cars you may recognize from the movies. The museum boasts twenty-five galleries, and up to one hundred vehicles are on display at any given time. For a few dollars more, they let you into the exclusive underground vault containing many of the rarest cars and trucks in the collection. After your visit, you can peruse the parking lot to see future collections in the making.

BONUS FACT: Hip hop artist Notorious B.I.G. was killed just after leaving a party at the Petersen.

BEST TIME TO GO: Closes at 5:00 p.m.
PARKING: Look for a meter or free parking on 6th Street.

Chapter 5

HOTELS

Hotels aren't just for weary travelers looking for a place to stay for a night—they are often hubs of important activity. Before the city was built up, hotels were some of the first places prospective residents could come to congregate. Over the years, they have served as the sites of scandals, outrageous parties, ghost stories and even assassinations. Sure an Airbnb can be less expensive, but if you do need to actually utilize a hotel for spending the night, it can be quite exciting to sleep where something controversial or exciting happened. There are many great hotels around, but here are a few with a bit of fun history I like to point out.

The Hollywood Roosevelt

7000 Hollywood Boulevard, Los Angeles, CA 90028

Still active hotel known for celebrity ghosts.

As LA's oldest continuously operating hotel and located smack dab in the middle of the Hollywood Walk of Fame, the Roosevelt hotel has seen more than its share of Hollywood happenings. Its connections to the movie business go back to the beginning. Early Hollywood titans Douglas Fairbanks, Mary Pickford and Louis B. Mayer were among the hotel's initial investors. The first Academy Awards ceremony was held in the ballroom in 1929. It was not the lavish affair we know today, but the tradition has been brought back full

The Hollywood Roosevelt is the oldest continuously operating hotel in Los Angeles and the location of the first Academy Awards. *Adam Papagan.*

circle since the current home of the Oscars is just across the street. Various renovations through the years have covered up and then restored the hotel's historic elements, but a visit today is like a trip back in time.

It should also be mentioned that the hotel is haunted by at least three famous ghosts. Montgomery Clift lived in the hotel while making the movie *From Here to Eternity*, and it's said that you can hear his ghosts reciting lines from the movie. Errol Flynn, who is rumored to have invented a recipe for bootleg gin in the hotel's barbershop, is also said to have made his ghostly presence known. The most famous ghost haunting the Roosevelt is Marilyn Monroe, who lived at the hotel for a few years and did her first major photoshoot by the pool. Of course, Marilyn is essentially the mascot of Hollywood and is believed to haunt many establishments on the Boulevard, so I'm not sure how much time her ghost actually spends here.

BEST TIME TO GO: Word is they won't let people hang around if they're not guests, so look like you know where you're going.
PARKING: Park at the mall across the street. It's a few dollars with validation obtained from the mall.

The Beverly Hills Hotel

9641 Sunset Boulevard, Beverly Hills, CA 90210

Beverly Hills' social epicenter.

The Beverly Hills Hotel has been at the center of Beverly Hills life since before the city was even founded. The hotel was built to entice potential residents and even served as a de facto city hall in the town's early days. It officially opened in 1912 and quickly became associated with the burgeoning movie industry. Silent film stars Douglas Fairbanks and Mary Pickford were early patrons. Elizabeth Taylor spent six of her eight honeymoons here. The exterior is also featured on the Eagles' *Hotel California* album cover. The hotel's restaurant, the Polo Lounge, is still a place where you can reliably spot celebrities seven days a week. I once saw Dr. Phil in the bathroom, which is another tip—the bathroom in the lobby is the best in LA.

BEST TIME TO GO: Around mealtimes, you're most likely to see celebrities coming and going from the Polo Lounge.
PARKING: Street parking on North Crescent Drive. Enter the hotel via the side entrance by the bungalows.

The Beverly Hilton

9876 Wilshire Boulevard, Beverly Hills, CA 90210

Upscale hotel known for award shows and scandal.

Situated at the western entrance to Beverly Hills and its proximity to celebrities, the Beverly Hilton has been the location of several infamous events. Since 1961, the International Ballroom has hosted the Golden Globes ceremony, which recently came under boycott for its long history of racist or exclusionary practices. Senator and U.S. presidential candidate John Edwards was videotaped visiting his mistress, Rielle Hunter, at the hotel during his extramarital affair scandal in 2007. In 2012, singer Whitney Houston drowned in the bathroom of suite 434. This is also the location of Richard Nixon's 1962 "last press conference," where he lashed out at reporters, saying, "You won't have Nixon to kick around anymore." Within a decade, he would be embroiled in the Watergate scandal.

Judy Garland and John F. Kennedy attending an event at the Beverly Hilton. *U.S. News and World Report.*

BEST TIME TO GO: It's easiest to poke around during the day.
PARKING: It has its own structure and there's two-hour parking in the streets off Wilshire, but this is just a drive-by.

AMBASSADOR HOTEL

3400 Wilshire Boulevard, Los Angeles, CA 90005

Former site of a swanky hotel and nightclub, a political assassination and now a public school.

After declaring victory in the California primary in a speech to supporters, Senator Robert F. Kennedy was shot by crazed assassin Sirhan Sirhan in the pantry area of the kitchen of the Ambassador Hotel.

Aside from being the location of one of the most significant events of 1968—the same year that saw the assassination of Martin Luther King, the height of the Vietnam War and the release of the *White Album*—the Ambassador Hotel had already been a notable LA hotspot for decades. Opened in 1921 with a one-thousand-room capacity, the hotel was frequented by celebrities like Charlie Chaplin, Lucille Ball and Carole Lombard. Its in-house nightclub, the Cocoanut Grove, was one of the city's premier performance venues, hosting concerts by Frank Sinatra, Peggy Lee and Nat King Cole. Despite closing to guests in 1989, the hotel remained an active filming location for years for the likes of *Forrest Gump*, *Almost Famous* and *Roy Orbison & Friends: A Night in Black and White*. After being acquired by the Los Angeles Unified School District, most of the original building was demolished in 2005. Today, it is Robert F. Kennedy Community Schools and is closed to the public.

BEST TIME TO GO: Preferably not when school's in session, but what's left of the building is easily viewable from Wilshire Boulevard.

PARKING: Parking is always tough in K-town, but there might be something off one of the side streets. You can also pull up quickly on Wilshire Boulevard to grab a picture.

Sunset Tower Hotel

8358 Sunset Boulevard, West Hollywood, CA 90069

Clandestine celebrity meet-up spot.

The Sunset Tower opened in 1931 and is considered one of the best and most ornate examples of Art Deco architecture in Los Angeles. The building was designed by Leland Bryant, who designed many large, chateau-inspired apartment buildings during this period. The Sunset Tower was built as an apartment hotel specifically to cater to celebrity clientele. Former residents include John Wayne, Howard Hughes and Frank Sinatra, all known for throwing decadent parties in the tower's penthouse. Wealthy men were said to rent apartments at the tower for their girlfriends and mistresses. According to Truman Capote, a former resident, the hotel was where "every scandal that ever

The Sunset Tower Hotel was built in an Art Deco style. *Carol Highsmith.*

happened happened." Like everything hip in Hollywood, the Sunset Tower eventually fell in popularity and entered a period of decline. A twenty-first-century redesign and renaming to the Argyle has once again made it a go-to celebrity hangout.

BEST TIME TO GO: If you can get a day pass to the pool, it is a great scene.
PARKING: Parking is really hard to find on this part of the Strip, but you may have good fortune with a meter.

Andaz West Hollywood (The "Riot House")

6363 Sunset Boulevard, Los Angeles, CA 90028

Hard-partying Sunset Strip staple.

The Andaz Hotel, formerly the Continental Hyatt House and affectionately nicknamed the "Riot House," was a regular site for touring rock bands in the '70s. Led Zeppelin would rent up to six floors at a time for band members and their entourage. Legend has it that they once rode motorcycles up and down the halls. Music's wildest Keiths (Richards and Moon) both reportedly threw TVs off the balconies of their rooms. Today, the balconies are enclosed in glass, possibly for this very reason. The hotel was also Little Richards' longtime home, and part of *This Is Spinal Tap* was filmed on the roof. The name changed to the Andaz in 2009, but it is still a hip spot, occasionally popping up on the reality shows *The Real Housewives of Beverly Hills* and *Vanderpump Rules*. The hotel's Riot House restaurant pays homage to the hotel's former nickname.

BEST TIME TO GO: Book a day pass for the rooftop for some of the best views of the Hollywood Hills in the city.
PARKING: Few good parking options exist on the Strip, but the hotel has a valet.

Chateau Marmont

8221 Sunset Boulevard, Los Angeles, CA 90046

Spooky and secretive celebrity hangout.

The Chateau Marmont is stationed like a fortress at the eastern edge of the Sunset Strip. The hotel has long been known as both a long- and short-term residence for celebrities on their way up and down the ladder of fame. Famously, the hotel was the site of comedian John Belushi's accidental overdose in 1982. Over its long history, the hotel has gained a reputation as a place for celebrities to either work, have affairs or go on benders. Because of this, the staff has grown accustomed to protecting the privacy of their guests, so play it cool if you go. Currently, there are talks of turning the entire property into a private club, so be prepared for it to get a lot more exclusive.

BEST TIME TO GO: Day or night, the vibe is very exclusionary.
PARKING: Not a lot of options if you don't want to valet. Your best bet is probably to look for parking east of Crescent Heights and walk over.

SUNSET MARQUIS HOTEL

1200 Alta Loma Road, West Hollywood, CA 90069

Classic rock star stomping ground that still occasionally rocks.

The Sunset Marquis is an old-school rock star hangout where you still might find some old rock stars hanging out. The hotel, tucked into a hidden cul-de-sac just steps from the Sunset Strip, opened in 1963 specifically to cater to the hard-partying entertainment industry. The permissive atmosphere and inexpensive rooms made it popular with touring musicians and rock stars in town to record an album or play a show, and it quickly became a headquarters of sorts for rock-and-roll. Gradually, the hotel became more and more chic, and today, it is essentially a modern boutique hotel. It's still very faithful to the vibe, however. The lobby is home to the Morrison Hotel Gallery, which specializes in rock photography. Work from the gallery is used to decorate the hotel, with photographs of musicians like Joe Strummer lounging by the Sunset Marquis pool. It also still hosts music industry events and parties. An event to honor the fiftieth anniversary of the Doors album *Morrison Hotel* featured guitarist Robbie Krieger performing songs from the album with celebrity guests. Jim Morrison never showed up, but it was still a wild night.

BEST TIME TO GO: Many Grammy Award nominees stay at the hotel when they're in town for the awards, so you never know who you might spot in the lobby.

PARKING: There's sometimes parking on Holloway during the day. At night, it's permit only, so read the signs.

Beverly Wilshire Hotel

9500 Wilshire Boulevard, Beverly Hills, CA 90212

Exclusive accommodations with some odd touches.

Another one of Beverly Hills' famous hotels is the Beverly Wilshire. The hotel was completed in 1928 on the former site of the Beverly Hills Speedway. John Lennon, Warren Beatty and Elvis Presley all lived here at different points. It's also the setting of the film *Pretty Woman*, although most of the interiors were shot at the nearby Ambassador Hotel. Behind the main building are full-scale replicas of the Buckingham Palace gates, an El Camino Real bell and lamps modeled after those found in Edinburgh, Scotland, which go largely unnoticed by most guests. Strange but fitting for a weird little town like Beverly Hills.

BEST TIME TO GO: During the day. In the morning, you'll see lots of fancy cars arriving.

PARKING: The City of Beverly Hills operates a free two-hour lot on Canon Drive.

Millennium Biltmore

506 South Grand Avenue, Los Angeles, CA 90071

Long-running downtown institution and frequent filming location.

The Millennium Biltmore Hotel is a touch of old-world class in the rapidly changing Downtown LA. The 1923 building is lavishly adorned in frescos and murals, marble fountains and crystal chandeliers. The hotel has the usual show business connections for a building of its age in Los Angeles. Many of the early Academy Awards ceremonies were held here. It's also been a filming location for *They Live!*, *A Star Is Born*, *Ocean's 11*, *Mad Men*,

Wedding Crashers, *The West Wing*, *Fight Club* and *That '70s Show*. This is also one of the last places Black Dahlia Elizabeth Short was rumored to have been seen.

BEST TIME TO GO: If you're just stopping by for a visit, do it while you're seeing other things downtown.
PARKING: Few meters in this area, even for downtown. You'll have to park at the hotel or a nearby lot.

InterContinental Los Angeles Downtown

900 Wilshire Boulevard, Los Angeles, CA 90017

The West's highest hotel.

Los Angeles was built out, not up, so for a city this large, there aren't that many tall buildings. Officially, the tallest building in Los Angeles is Wilshire Grand Center—kind of. They did that thing where they added a spire to the top to increase the height. The U.S. Bank building down the street is at a higher elevation, making its top floors higher than the Wilshire Grand, but you can't go up there. Wilshire Grand's InterContinental Hotel occupies most of the building, with its lobby on the seventieth floor. It also has rooftop bar called Spire 73, which is the highest open-air platform on the West Coast. I'll have to take their word for it. This is also where I discovered I have an intense fear of heights. I didn't make it past the elevator.

BEST TIME TO GO: Check the hours for the rooftop bar. That's the main attraction.
PARKING: There's an underground lot for the hotel that you pretty much have to park in.

The Westin Bonaventure

404 South Figueroa Street, Los Angeles, CA 90071

Imposing downtown hotel tower with futuristic flourishes.

Architecture people and urban theorists love to go on about the Westin Bonaventure Hotel. It was designed by architect and real estate developer

The futuristic Westin Bonaventure hotel was featured in the movie *Blade Runner*. *Carol Highsmith.*

John C. Portman Jr. in 1974. Portman popularized hotels built around large indoor atriums. You may have been to one in San Francisco, New York, Detroit or Atlanta. The Bonaventure is the epitome of postmodern—an indoor space that feels outside, overly planned but also disorienting to visitors, representing a revitalized downtown that's stoic and empty. It is all of those things but also just a cool retro-futuristic hotel that's fun to explore. The floating concrete seating areas and designated indoor running track make it feel like something out of *Logan's Run*. In fact, many future-set films have been shot at the Bonaventure, including *Blade Runner*, *Xanadu* and *Escape from L.A.* Even if you're not into all that architecture stuff, the hotel is still worth a visit if you're in the area, even if the layout is a bit odd.

BEST TIME TO GO: It's always sort of empty, but around lunchtime on weekdays, the Downtown LA office workers provide good people-watching.

PARKING: There is hardly any street parking in this area, not even meters. The best bet is to park at the hotel or walk over after visiting somewhere else.

Hollywood Knickerbocker Hotel

1714 Ivar Avenue, Los Angeles, CA 90028

Likely haunted former hotel with decades' long history of celebrity connections.

In a town known for endless sprawl, it's still amazing how jam-packed Hollywood is with obscure and esoteric locations. The Hollywood Knickerbocker Hotel opened in 1929 and is the site of numerous Hollywood triumphs and tragedies. Elvis Presley stayed here while making his first Hollywood film, *Love Me Tender*. In 1936, the widow of magician Harry Houdini conducted her tenth séance to contact her late husband on the roof of the hotel. There is now a permanent Houdini Séance room at the Magic Castle less than a mile away. Pioneering silent film director D.W. Griffith dropped dead in the lobby in 1948, as did character actor William Frawley (Fred from *I Love Lucy*) nearly twenty years later. Stooge Larry Fine also lived here for a number of years. As the Hollywood neighborhood began to decline, so did the hotel, and it was sold in the early 1970s. Today, the building is low-income housing for senior citizens, a rare positive turn for such an infamous property. It is closed to the public.

BEST TIME TO GO: Not much to see here, but in the morning, you can watch Scientologists arrive for work at the Sea Org down the street.

PARKING: Metered street parking.

Chapter 6

FILM, TV AND MUSIC

The movie business isn't LA's only industry. The region has one of the densest concentrations of manufacturing in America. We're also home to one of the busiest ports in the world in San Pedro and Long Beach. California's number one industry as a whole is still agriculture. But show business is maybe LA's most magical industry. The imaginative stories crafted here and presented through this medium go on to become a part of American heritage and influence people and events worldwide. The amazing thing is that you can actually visit many of the places where this happens every day. The city abounds with soundstages, recording studios and free-standing sets where Hollywood's next biggest moments are being created.

Lasky-DeMille Barn

2100 North Highland Avenue, Los Angeles, CA 90068

LA's first film studio, located in an old barn.

There was once a time way back in history when Hollywood had no movie studios at all. The very first was the Lasky-DeMille Barn, an unassuming building originally located at the corner of Selma and Vine. The barn was rented by partners Jesse Lasky and Cecil B. DeMille to produce their 1914 film *The Squaw Man*. As legend has it, the film, a western, was originally slated to be shot in Flagstaff, Arizona. DeMille found the mountainous

This barn was used to film scenes for the first feature film shot entirely in Los Angeles. *Adam Papagan.*

terrain unsuitable for his vision, and the whole crew soon piled back on the train, eventually arriving in California. Here, they found sunshine, cheap land and a variety of easily accessible, varied filming locations. *The Squaw Man* became the first feature film shot in Hollywood, and an industry was born. The building was declared a state historic landmark in 1956 and was moved to several different locations before settling in its current spot in the Hollywood Bowl parking lot. It's open to visitors on the weekends as the Hollywood Heritage Museum, which displays artifacts from the silent era and occasionally hosts film screenings and events.

BEST TIME TO GO: Open only on weekends.
PARKING: Free parking in front.

Charlie Chaplin Studios

1416 North La Brea Avenue, Los Angeles, CA 90028

The original studio of one of Hollywood's most recognizable stars and later home of the Muppets.

For more than a century, Charlie Chaplin has loomed large over Hollywood. Nearly every establishment in the city that opened before World War II will mention Chaplin when rattling off their list of famous former patrons, whether he actually spent much time there or not. One place he definitely would have spent time is his film studio on La Brea and Sunset. Chaplin built the original studio in 1919 in the style of a picturesque village in his native England. Some of his best-known films—including *City Lights*, *The Kid* and *The Great Dictator*—were filmed here. Chaplin sold the property in 1953, where it was used to film *The Adventures of Superman* and later became the headquarters of A&M Records. There's still a recording studio on the property, which is where the all-star hit "We Are the World" was recorded. Later, the complex became home to the Jim Henson Company, which placed a large statue of a mustachioed Kermit the Frog holding a cane and bowler hat on the roof as an homage to Chaplin. The studio's latest owners are musician John Mayer and producer McG. Near the front gate, there's a segment of cement containing Charlie Chaplin's signature and footprints, but they are allegedly a re-creation, another tangential connection. Other than that, the studio is not open to the public.

BEST TIME TO GO: Daytime.
PARKING: Meters on La Brea and restricted parking on some of the side streets.

20TH Century Studios

10201 West Pico Boulevard, Los Angeles, CA 90064

Major film studio with hidden throwback entrance.

Most of your favorite movies and TV shows were filmed in big, empty buildings scattered across Los Angeles. The Fox Lot (now called 20th Century Studios since its acquisition by Disney in 2019) was once one of the Big Six major movie studios and has a history similar to that of its counterparts—a right-place-at-the-right-time founder, periods of expansion and decline, ownership changes and some celebrity name dropping for good measure. What makes the Fox property special are the old studio gates around the corner from the Pico entrance. Head north three blocks on Fox Hills Drive around the perimeter of the studio and you'll come to the original Art Deco gates hidden at the end of a residential street. It's easy to see some of the old buildings through the bars of the gates and soundstages beyond. The little window to the left is where movie extras used to get paid at the end of the day. You can almost see the line of starry-eyed hopefuls queued up for a chance at their big break, back when the movie business used to be something you could walk right up to.

BEST TIME TO GO: On weekdays, it's busier, and you can watch studio employees coming and going.
PARKING: The main gate is inhospitable to cars and pedestrians, but head over to the side gate on Fox Hills Drive for a better view.

PARAMOUNT STUDIOS

5515 Melrose Avenue, Los Angeles, CA 90038

The only public tour of a Hollywood studio actually in Hollywood.

The Paramount Studio Tour is less theme park-y than some of the other studio tours around town. Instead, the focus is on the (mostly accurate) history of the company, as well as the day-to-day operations of the only major traditional studio left in Hollywood. The intimate tour (maximum of seven guests) starts out with you getting to hold a real Oscar. You then hop

Paramount is the last traditional film studio still located in Hollywood. *Carol Highsmith.*

on a golf cart, and a studio page drives you around the lot, regaling you with the history of the studio system, Cecil B. DeMille, Lucille Ball and other icons who have worked on the property over the years. There are also many opportunities to get out and explore (supervised, of course) actual movie sets and the prop house. Honestly, it's just a bunch of buildings, but folks on the tour were loving every minute. At the end, one lady remarked, "I'll never look at movies the same way again." I'm not sure how she thought movies were made going into the tour, but now she knows a little bit more about how they do all that Hollywood stuff.

BEST TIME TO GO: Tours are offered every half hour. I try to get stuff like this out of the way in the morning.
PARKING: The lot they tell you to park in costs money. However, there is free street parking two blocks east of the studio.

Paramount Ranch

2903 Cornell Road, Agoura Hills, CA 91301

National park where westerns are filmed.

It's not uncommon for film studios to operate "movie ranches" filled with freestanding sets that can be used to film television shows and movies. What is uncommon is for one of those ranches to be a national park the public is allowed to visit. Paramount Movie Ranch was built to resemble an Old West town in 1923 and has been a filming location for everyone from Bob Hope to *Dr. Quinn* to *Westworld*. The property changed hands a few times but was eventually acquired by the National Park Service in 1980. The park service rents out the sets to production companies, but the rest of the time it is open to the public, where they are invited to roam the dusty streets and explore the empty buildings. The 2018 Woolsey Fire destroyed much of the ranch, but a chapel and train depot still remain, with plans to restore and reimagine the park for ongoing film production and the enjoyment of the public.

BEST TIME TO GO: Open 8:00 a.m. to 8:00 p.m. during the summer.
PARKING: Parking lot.

Walt Disney Studios

500 South Buena Vista Street, Burbank, CA 91521

Walt's workplace.

The Walt Disney Company is one of the largest and most successful media conglomerates in the history of entertainment. Its core business is still the movies. The studio property was built in 1940 using revenue from *Snow White and the Seven Dwarfs* and still houses many branches of the Disney empire, including Marvel, ABC, the animation department and high-level executive offices. In typical Disney fashion, many of the buildings are adorned with statues of well-known characters or references to their films. You can see the Seven Dwarfs carved into the front of the Michael D. Eisner Building from the street, and Mickey's giant sorcerer hat is easily visible from the 134 Freeway. Much of the "magic" people experience at the Disney Parks was conceived of right here. Since this is the only of the major studios not to offer a regular public tour, a certain mystique has been built up around it. Legend has it that Walt spent his final moments at the hospital just across the street, using the grid of the ceiling tiles to lay out his vision for Epcot.

BEST TIME TO GO: Tours are occasionally offered to members of the D23 fan club.
PARKING: Just pull over to get a quick picture.

Disney purchased its lot with money made from *Snow White and the Seven Dwarfs*. *Historic American Buildings Survey.*

Sony Pictures Tour

10202 Washington Boulevard, Culver City, CA 90232

Studio tour scant on history but heavy with intellectual property.

Much of what is now Sony Pictures was acquired from Columbia TriStar. The Sony Tour focuses less on history and more on associating the studio with *Jeopardy*, *Shark Tank*, *Seinfeld*, *The Goldbergs* (lots of Goldbergs), *Breaking Bad* and your other favorite Sony-connected properties. However, the lot where most of those things were produced is over in Hollywood. The physical space in Culver City Sony now occupies was once the mighty MGM, but most of that company was sold off piece by piece long ago. The result is that the Sony Tour is more akin to a standard factory tour depicting the actual day-to-day work of a major movie studio. The tour takes you into a few unused soundstages and recording studios where your college-aged tour guide recounts inoffensive anecdotes carefully crafted specifically for their tourist audience. There's nothing here about Masaru Ibuka or Akio Morita, the founders of the Sony Corporation. They take you by a soundstage where a hit show is being filmed, with no mention that one of its biggest stars was recently fired for sexual misconduct. Nothing about the 2014 North Korean hack either.

At fifty dollars per person, it's significantly cheaper than some of the other studio tour options. At the end of the tour, every guest receives a complimentary souvenir photo of themselves green-screened onto the *Jeopardy* set. You don't actually get to visit the *Jeopardy* set, but you get a photo of what it would be like if you really did. In a strange way, it's as true to Hollywood as anything you experience on the tour. It's never about the thing, just what people associate with it.

BEST TIME TO GO: The summers are brutally hot, so keep that in mind. The earlier tours seem to be less crowded, but they really pack them in here.
PARKING: FREE VALET PARKING!

Warner Bros. Studios Tour

3400 Warner Boulevard, Burbank, CA 91505

See how movies are made and visit an iconic water tower.

The Warner Bros. tour is actually pretty good. The history of Warner Bros. is pretty standard for a place like this and not all that uniquely interesting in and of itself, but they do a good job of making it theme park-y and entertaining. After sitting through an intro video hosted by Ellen DeGeneres, they split guests into small groups, and a live guide frantically ushers you around the lot in a golf cart. I got the impression there is no set route, and the guides are told just to kill time for about an hour, which added an unpredictable element that was kind of exciting. The second half of the tour mostly consists of a *Friends* exhibit/restaurant/retail environment that is totally overstimulating but a must for any superfan. Much of the strength of the WB tour can be attributed to its superior intellectual property. With DC Comics, Harry Potter, *Gilmore Girls* and Looney Tunes, there's something the whole family will want to see. This is the only one of the studio tours I went on that was actually sort of fun.

BEST TIME TO GO: They hustle a lot of people through here, so you can usually get on a tour within minutes of showing up.
PARKING: There's a fifteen-dollar lot but also plenty of free parking on the adjacent streets.

Universal Studios

100 Universal City Plaza, Universal City, CA 91608

A movie studio with its own theme park, or a theme park with its own movie studio.

Unlike Disneyland, the Universal Studios theme park is located on the grounds of an actual functioning movie studio. Inviting the public to see how movies are made was always part of Universal's original plan. When the studio opened in 1914, founder Carl Laemmle charged spectators five cents (which included a chicken lunch) to observe the moviemaking process. When sound films became the norm in the '30s, this proved to be impractical, and the studio tour was nixed. However, a revamped studio tour began operating in 1964. Over the decades, it evolved into the full-blown theme park we know today, featuring rides dedicated to *The Simpsons*, *Jurassic Park*, *The Mummy* and *Minions*. The star attraction remains the studio tour. In my opinion, Universal is not as good as Disneyland, but it's closer, a little less expensive and small enough to see in one day, making it a much more practical option for many.

BEST TIME TO GO: If you get there when it opens, it's less crowded and less hot, plus you'll have enough time to do something else later in the day.
PARKING: You pretty much have to park in the parking structure. There's free street parking a few blocks south of Ventura Boulevard off Lankershim, but it's quite a trek to the theme park gates.

Hollywood Walk of Fame

Hollywood Boulevard between La Brea and Gower

Famous sidewalk honoring thousands.

The red, black and gold stars of the Hollywood Walk of Fame are one of the most recognizable parts of Hollywood Boulevard, stretching over two miles down Hollywood between La Brea and Gower and for a few blocks north and south on Vine Street. The Walk of Fame tradition began back in 1960, honoring the pioneering entertainers and creatives of Hollywood's early days. After a period of stagnation, chamber of commerce president and Hollywood's honorary mayor Johnny Grant realized the Walk's power as a promotional tool and began to expand it. There are six official categories of stars: Film, TV, Radio, Music, Sports Entertainment and Live Performance. A performer can receive stars in multiple categories, but before Sports was added in 2023, the only person with all five was singing cowboy Gene Autry (Bob Hope has four). If an honoree's nomination is approved by the chamber, they have to agree to show up to the unveiling if they're living and pay an induction fee, which is up to around $75,000. The chamber hosts as many as two Star Ceremonies per month, and today, there are over 2,700 stars on the Walk of Fame. As you walk down the sidewalk, you'll see many names you recognize and many more you will not. It's important to remember that at one point, all of these names were recognizable enough to be included on the Walk of Fame. Many cynical visitors will refer to Hollywood as the "Boulevard of Broken Dreams," but to me, this is the

When a celebrity dies, fans often leave tributes at their Walk of Fame stars. *Carol Highsmith.*

"Boulevard of Accomplished Dreams." Even if your chances of making it in entertainment are slim, here are the names of 2,700 people and counting who were able to do it before you.

BEST TIME TO GO: If you're just trying to see the stars, the streets are nearly deserted early in the morning.
PARKING: Easy street parking in the residential neighborhood west of La Brea. The cheapest lot is at the Hollywood and Highland Mall.

Dolby Theater

6801 Hollywood Boulevard, Hollywood, CA 90028

Home of the Oscars in an unlikely place.

They actually do the Oscars at the mall. The Dolby Theater (originally the Kodak Theater) has been the permanent home to the Academy Awards since

2002. The theater was built into the Ovation Hollywood mall specifically for this purpose. Every year, a few days before the award ceremony, the streets are blocked off, curtains are placed in front of the storefronts and the red carpet is rolled down the mall's central corridor. It looks much nicer on TV, but it's really just the mall. Other events are hosted at the Dolby Theater like the *American Idol* finale and the occasional concert or traveling stage production, but its main purpose is for the Academy Awards. I appreciate the Dolby because while other major events associated with Hollywood occurred decades ago, the Dolby is actively helping create modern show business history. This is where they accidentally gave the Oscar to *La La Land* instead of *Moonlight* and where Will Smith slapped Chris Rock. Who knows what else could happen? The Dolby has a contract to hold the awards until 2032, so long as the awards stay in Hollywood.

BEST TIME TO GO: If you're also going to the Chinese Theater and the Walk of Fame, it's worth popping over.
PARKING: The Ovation Hollywood shopping center, where the theater is located, has the largest parking garage in Los Angeles.

CBS Television City

7800 Beverly Boulevard, Los Angeles, CA 90036

Production facility home to many favorites from years gone by.

Imagine it: an entire city dedicated to television. While not an actual municipality, Television City is home to the CBS television network's West Coast operations. Built in 1952, the facility has been home to countless productions, including *Dancing with the Stars*, *The Late Late Show*, *Card Sharks*,

CBS's West Coast headquarters is located on Beverly and Fairfax. *Carol Highsmith.*

Family Feud, *America's Got Talent*, *The Merv Griffin Show* and *The Young and the Restless*. My two buddies and I once spent a very long night camped out in front of Television City in order to attend Bob Barker's second-to-last taping of *The Price Is Right.* When we finally made it inside, it was like going inside the TV set. Maybe the name fits, after all.

BEST TIME TO GO: Television productions are desperate for people to sit in the studio audience. You can always get free tickets to TV show tapings, and sometimes you can even find situations where they pay *you* to attend. (Warning: Television production is painfully boring.)
PARKING: Street parking, but this is mainly a drive-by.

Jimmy Kimmel Live!
6840 Hollywood Boulevard, Los Angeles, CA 90028

Nightly television still produced on Hollywood Boulevard.

Although it's not as "Live!" as the name suggests, *Jimmy Kimmel Live!* is one of the few productions still regularly broadcasting from Hollywood Boulevard. Appearing on Kimmel, along with movie premieres and the yearly Oscars ceremony, is one of the only reasons a movie star would actually still come to Hollywood Boulevard. The show began airing in 2003. Prior to becoming a soundstage, the building was the location of the Hollywood Masonic Temple, so it has deep show business roots. Tickets to attend a taping are free, but if you want to try to get on camera, you can occasionally find producers roaming the sidewalk for unsuspecting tourists to feature in "Man on the Street" segments. Periodically, Kimmel will host Fan Appreciation days where he invites the public in for a photo op. One year, I just so happened to be giving a tour of the Boulevard on one of those days. I noted to my guests that this was their chance to get a picture with an actual celebrity during their visit to Hollywood. "No thanks," they said. "We watch Jimmy Fallon." What can I say? It's a tough town.

BEST TIME TO GO: Shows recorded daily.
PARKING: Hollywood and Highland Mall across the street.

PRETTY WOMAN APARTMENT

1738 Las Palmas Avenue, Los Angeles, CA 90028

Famous rom-com rendezvous location.

While the story may be a little unbelievable, many of the filming locations were real places. The apartment where Julia Roberts's character lived is the old Las Palmas Hotel. The view of the building from Hollywood Boulevard is now partially blocked by a new high-rise, so you'll have to walk about a half block up from the main drag to get a good view. If you look closely, you can spot a mural of the two embracing on the fire escape painted in the building's laundry room. A visit will also confirm that the building actually is a seedy motel in real life too.

The building used as Julia Roberts's apartment in *Pretty Woman* is actually a seedy motel in real life too. *Adam Papagan.*

BEST TIME TO GO: Mornings and midday Hollywood is less crazy.
PARKING: Meters and street parking on Las Palmas.

FRANKLIN CANYON

2600 Franklin Canyon Drive, Beverly Hills, CA 90210

Immersive natural landscape minutes from the Valley.

Nestled exactly between the hustle and bustle of Ventura Boulevard and the posh boutiques of Rodeo Drive is rustic Franklin Canyon Park. The lake at the park was once used as a reservoir, but its woodsy vibe and accessibility from Hollywood quickly made it an ideal filming location. Claudette Colbert's famous hitchhiking scene from *It Happened One Night* was filmed here as far back as 1935. The opening to *The Andy Griffith Show* was too. Simon and Garfunkel and the Rolling Stones also used the park for album cover shoots. Today, about twenty-five film shoots happen here annually, but locals mostly enjoy it for the five miles of hiking trails and a little slice of nature in the precise geographic center of metro Los Angeles.

BEST TIME TO GO: Open from sunrise to sunset.
PARKING: Free

Vasquez Rocks

10700 Escondido Canyon Road, Agua Dulce, CA 91390

An alien planet minutes from the highway.

For decades, the distinctive rock formations known as Vasquez Rocks have been a stand-in for far-off alien worlds, as well as prehistoric villages and freewheeling western towns. The rocks are named for Mexican bandito Tiburcio Vásquez, who hid there to avoid capture, which itself sounds like something out of a movie. Vasquez Rocks are featured in no fewer than four episodes of the original *Star Trek* series. They also pop up in *The Flintstones*, *Zorro*, *The Muppet Movie* and countless commercials. Vasquez Rocks are a bit outside of the city but a lot closer than trying to get to outer space.

BEST TIME TO GO: Closed at night.
PARKING: They have a lot.

Bronson Canyon

3200 Canyon Drive, Los Angeles, CA 90068

A short canyon hike to exotic worlds.

One of the things that initially attracted filmmakers to Los Angeles was the variety of exotic filming locations contained within the city's borders. Travel just a few miles from Hollywood Boulevard and you could find yourself on Clipper Island (*Robinson Crusoe of Clipper Island*, 1936), ancient Egypt (*The Scorpion King*, 2002) or even the mysterious Planet Arous (*The Brain From Planet Arous*, 1957). In actuality, all of these places (and more!) were the caves of

Bronson Canyon. Located just north of busy Franklin Avenue, the caves have been a familiar Hollywood backdrop since the silent era. Movies and TV shows filmed in the caves include *Star Trek*, *George of the Jungle*, *The A-Team*, *Gunsmoke*, *Mighty Morphin Power Rangers*, *Invasion of the Body Snatchers*, *The Searchers* and *The Monkees.* The area was originally used as a quarry, which created its unique caves and rock formations. The main cave is large enough to drive a car through, which came in handy when it was the location of the Batcave of the original *Batman* television series. Unfortunately, they won't let you drive your car through it, but it's still a fun, easy hike nonetheless.

BEST TIME TO GO: Daytime, as it closes after dark.
PARKING: Free parking lot.

Marilyn Monroe

12305 5th Helena Drive, Los Angeles, CA 90049

Physical places associated with LA's ultimate icon.

Marilyn Monroe is the de facto "mascot" of Hollywood. *Carol Highsmith.*

Decades after her death, Marilyn Monroe still remains a quintessential Los Angeles icon and symbol of the twin triumphs and tragedy of success. This was Marilyn's final home. In 2024, under threat of imminent demolition, the Los Angeles City Council swiftly swept in and declared the property an official historic landmark because it was the first home Monroe sought out and purchased for herself.

Marilyn was a SoCal native and moved around a lot, so there are literally dozens of locations associated with her around the county. Her childhood home was in Hawthorne (*4201 West 134th Street*), she attended school at West LA's University High (*11800 Texas Avenue*) and her ghost is said to haunt the Roosevelt Hotel (*7000 Hollywood Boulevard*). Given her status as the effective mascot of Hollywood, her likeness is incorporated into as many attractions as possible, no matter how precarious the connection. A souvenir store on the corner of Hollywood and Highland features a mural of Marilyn and James Dean hanging out together, even though the two never met in real life. Look anywhere, and the spirit of Marilyn Monroe is all around, simultaneously as a warning of the pitfalls of fame and beckoning aspiring dreamers.

BEST TIME TO GO: The homes and school are closed to the public.
PARKING: Street parking.

Sunset Sound Recorders

6650 Sunset Boulevard, Los Angeles, CA 90028

Classic recording studio still going strong.

It's amazing that some of the most successful, influential albums of all time were recorded in nondescript, windowless buildings around Los Angeles. More than two hundred gold records were recorded here at Sunset Sound, including works by Guns N' Roses, Linda Ronstadt, the Beach Boys, the Rolling Stones, Led Zeppelin, Idina Menzel and Van Halen. They won't let you go inside, but the big, loopy psychedelic sign alone is worth a photo.

BEST TIME TO GO: Not open to the public.
PARKING: There's almost always metered parking in front or at the 711 next door if you're just popping over for a photo.

RCA West

6363 Sunset Boulevard, Los Angeles, CA 90028

Obscure building that created some of the biggest songs of the '60s.

Los Angeles had a booming music industry in the 1960s, with state-of-the-art recording studios all over Hollywood. Places like Goldstar and Capitol Records are more famous, but an equally important studio was RCA West, located at the corner of Sunset and Vine. Elvis recorded some of the songs from his movies here, as did the Monkees and the Grateful Dead, but its main contribution to music history is being the location where many of the Rolling Stones' biggest hits of the '60s were recorded. Although the Stones are British, some of their most innovative numbers were recorded in Los Angeles,

Many of the biggest hits of the '60s were recorded at RCA's Los Angeles studio. *Adam Papagan.*

including "Let's Spend the Night Together," "19th Nervous Breakdown" and "Satisfaction." The next time you hear that iconic riff, remember that the British Invasion was at least partially crafted in Hollywood.

BEST TIME TO GO: This is the campus of the Los Angeles Film School now, so you can't get past the lobby of the building.
PARKING: This one is primarily a drive-by.

Capitol Records

1750 Vine Street, Los Angeles, CA 90028

The last major record company left in Hollywood.

The iconic Capitol Records Building, built in 1955, is one of the most instantly recognizable parts of the Hollywood skyline. The building's

A mural depicting well-known musicians who recorded at the Capitol Records studio. *Adam Papagan.*

circular, Space Age design stands out among the other Art Deco and Spanish Revival buildings along the Boulevard. Many believe that the building is designed to resemble a stack of records with a phonograph needle on the top, although the building's architect maintained that the similarities were purely coincidental. The recording studio, famous for its eight subterranean echo chambers, has been used by everyone from Frank Sinatra to the Beach

Boys to Imagine Dragons. The building is also a popular target in disaster movies, having been destroyed in the films *Independence Day* and *The Day After Tomorrow*. The building itself is not open to the public.

BEST TIME TO GO: Each holiday season, the "needle" becomes the base of a giant Christmas tree on top of the building.
PARKING: Street parking.

Guitar Center RockWalk

7425 Sunset Boulevard, Los Angeles, CA 90046

Celebrity handprints not found at the Chinese Theater.

The handprints at the Chinese Theater have been imitated many times but never more enjoyably for music fans than at Guitar Center's RockWalk. Begun in 1985 at the retailer's flagship Hollywood store, the RockWalk honors notable musicians, instrument makers and music industry figures. Unlike the Chinese Theater, which mainly honors household names, the inductees to the RockWalk are much more eclectic. Here you can see the handprints of the architects of rock-and-roll, like Chuck Berry and Bo Diddley, alongside those of the surviving members of the legendary LA punk band the Germs. There's also a tribute to the Wrecking Crew, the session musicians who actually played on your favorite records by the Byrds, the Mamas and the Papas and the Monkees. The display cases around the courtyard also feature a rotating display of famous music gear like Eddie Van Halen's "Frankenstrat" guitar. It's worth it to take a stroll around the inside of the store, too. The Vintage Room in the back features an amazing inventory of rare guitars and equipment.

The RockWalk features the handprints of legendary musicians. *Adam Papagan.*

BEST TIME TO GO: Open during Guitar Center business hours.
PARKING: Guitar Center has its own lot. The entrance is off Sunset.

The Office
13927 Saticoy Street, Panorama City, CA 91402

The real location of the Rust Belt workplace.

Somehow around 2019 or so, the American version of *The Office* seemingly became everyone's favorite show. Los Angeles' answer to Scranton, Pennsylvania, is actually Panorama City, and much of the show was filmed in and around the San Fernando Valley. The Dunder Mifflin office/warehouse is, in reality, Valley Center Studios. There's no fancy set or anything. It's literally just a building at the studio. The average passerby may think that it's just another office building in the midst of Valley sprawl, but fans know it's actually *the* office. The studio is closed to the public.

BEST TIME TO GO: During regular business hours. Security is definitely tired of people coming to take pictures.
PARKING: Street parking.

A nondescript studio stands in for the nondescript workplace from *The Office*. *Adam Papagan.*

*M*A*S*H* Set

Malibu Creek State Park

Ruins of a classic TV, left in a state park.

The finale of the TV series *M*A*S*H* was watched by more than 121 million people and was one of the most viewed television programs up to that time. The show, a dramedy about a team of doctors in the Korean War, ran for eleven seasons, eight years longer than the conflict it was supposed to be depicting. Many of the exterior (outside in show business talk) shots were filmed at a movie ranch in Malibu owned by 20th Century Fox. The equipment ran on mobile generators and water was trucked in, not unlike a real field operation. When the show ended, many set pieces and rusted-out military vehicles were simply left behind. The land was eventually sold off and became Malibu Creek State Park. Park officials elected to keep the *M*A*S*H* set in place. Even if you're not a huge fan of the show, the hike is beautiful and a chance to explore a bit of television history for yourself.

BEST TIME TO GO: Open roughly sun up to sundown.
PARKING: Street parking, then it's an easy hike to set.

The Brady Bunch House

11222 Dilling Street, Studio City, CA 91602

One of TV's most iconic homes come to life.

Here's the story…of a house in the Valley that became a part of television history. When producers of the hit 1970s sitcom *The Brady Bunch* were looking for a home for the fictional blended family, they settled on this unassuming house on Dilling Street. The show was not actually filmed inside the house at all but rather on a soundstage at nearby Paramount Studios. Nevertheless, the home instantly became an icon. Over the years, the real owners grew tired of fans stopping by to take pictures and remodeled away the house's original retro charm with a wall and a new paint job. When the Brady house finally hit the market again in 2018, television network HGTV sensed a programming opportunity and purchased the house as the subject of a new show, *A Very Brady Renovation*. The interior and exterior

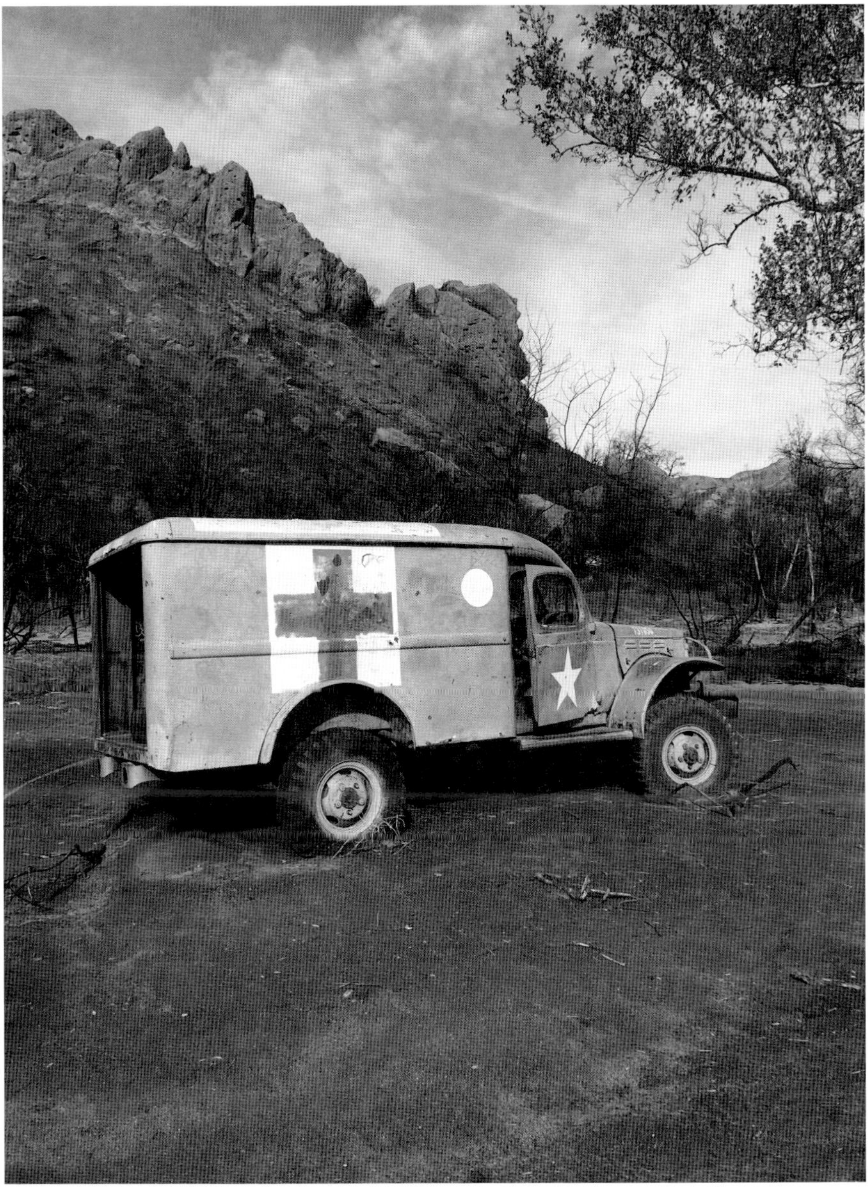

After the filming of the series, the set pieces for the show *M*A*S*H* were left behind in Malibu. *Adam Papagan.*

were transformed to look exactly how they would have appeared on the show, including adding a second floor where there was none before. The house is still owned by the production company and sits empty, guarded by an alert security guard twenty-four hours a day, so it is not open to the public. Fantasy becomes reality becomes fantasy becomes reality thanks to the magic of television.

BEST TIME TO GO: Daytime.
PARKING: Street parking.

Chapter 7

ENTERTAINMENT

There's no shortage of things to do here. Much of the entertainment industry is based in Los Angeles, so it's no surprise that we're blessed with the best movie theaters in the country, top-notch music venues big and small and nearly a dozen professional sports teams. Many of them also come with some bonus fun history and factoids. This chapter covers venues, performance spaces and arenas where you're likely to find world-class entertainment any night of the week.

Grauman's Chinese Theater

6925 Hollywood Boulevard, Hollywood, CA 90028

Still operational movie theater with celebrity handprints.

The most famous movie theater in the world (okay, there are not that many famous movie theaters) is Hollywood's Chinese Theater. Built in 1927 by impresario Sid Grauman, the most notable feature of the theater is its collection of celebrity hand and footprints set into the cement in front of the building. There are a few urban legends about how the footprints came to be, but all of them basically maintain that it was an accident. While they were building the theater, somebody stepped in wet cement, and that inspired Grauman to have movie stars do the same. Unlike the sprawling Walk of Fame, there are far fewer spaces for the handprints, and most are for movie stars you probably will have heard of. The most visited are that of

The forecourt of Grauman's Chinese Theater is where the celebrity footprints are located. *Adam Papagan.*

Marilyn Monroe, where the pigment of the cement is nearly worn off from six decades of tourists placing their hands in Marilyn's imprint.

Each set tells a story, but my favorite two are at the eastern edge of the theater. When TCL (a Chinese company) bought the theater, they anticipated Chinese tourists visiting in droves. However, these tourists might not know all of the actors from Hollywood's Golden Age. They enlisted the help of Zhao Wei and Huang Xiaoming, two actors who are huge stars in Asia but mostly unknown in the West, to cast their hands and footprints in the forecourt. Now, every day when Chinese tourists visit, they fall to their knees and place their hands in the cement, just like people do with Marilyn. These additions have taken the tradition internationally. I know that someday, far in the future, space aliens will be able to visit the Chinese Theater and place their tentacles alongside the imprints of their favorite Martian actors.

The theater still shows first-run movies and regularly hosts red carpet premieres.

BEST TIME TO GO: It's the least crowded early morning right when the forecourt opens.

PARKING: Hollywood and Highland Mall.

Egyptian Theater

6712 Hollywood Boulevard, Los Angeles, CA 90028

Themed movie theater with many past lives.

Before the Chinese Theater, there was the Egyptian Theater. Sid Grauman originally planned for his second Los Angeles theater to have a Spanish Mission–style theming, but design plans were changed mid-construction to capitalize on the public's current fascination with the Tomb of Tutankhamun. Though not as famous as its successor, the Egyptian is notable for being the site of the first-ever Hollywood red carpet movie premiere for the film *Douglas Fairbanks in Robin Hood* on October 18, 1922. From 1998 to 2020, the theater was operated by the nonprofit American Cinematheque, which would host special screenings of rare and historic films. In 2020, the theater was acquired by Netflix, which renovated and reopened the theater to host screenings that will qualify its films for Oscar consideration.

BEST TIME TO GO: Special events are usually held at night.
PARKING: Parking really isn't as intimidating in Hollywood as people say. You can usually find free parking on side streets—just make sure to read posted signs.

El Capitan Theater

6838 Hollywood Boulevard, Los Angeles, CA 90028

Disney-operated movie house.

The El Capitan first opened in 1928 as a venue for live stage productions but transitioned to showing movies after the successful premiere of *Citizen Kane*. In the 1940s, it was given a modern remodel and operated as the Paramount Theater for many decades. In the late 1980s, the theater was acquired by the Walt Disney Company, which restored the El Capitan name and original grand Spanish Revival architecture. The theater is the location of most Disney movie premieres and typically only shows Disney movies, usually accompanied by a special pre-show and display of props and costumes in the lobby. This is an official Disney attraction, and the employees are considered Disney cast members. The El Capitan is a great option if you are short on time and can only afford or tolerate a few hours of "Disney Magic."

The Walt Disney Company renovated the El Capitan in 1989. *Carol Highsmith.*

BEST TIME TO GO: It regularly hosts special screenings of Star Wars and other classic Disney films.

PARKING: Hollywood and Highland Mall across the street.

The New Beverly

7165 Beverly Boulevard, Los Angeles, CA 90036

Old-school movie theater showing classic movies on film.

The New Beverly Cinema is a funky old movie theater just south of Hollywood that's a paradise for film nerds. Since the late '70s, the repertory theater has shown nightly double (and sometimes triple) features of rare, classic and cult films, presented on 35mm whenever possible. The curation is excellent, and every film shown has some significant history that makes it worth seeing, even if you haven't heard of it. Over the years, I've been able to catch everything from Kubrick to Grindhouse on the big screen. Much of the theater's cool factor can be attributed to director Quentin Tarantino, who purchased it in 2007. Tarantino often programs the films himself, and

The New Beverly Theater is a haven for lovers of classic B-movies. *Adam Papagan.*

many of the prints come from his personal collection. He does not take his position as steward of this community gem lightly and has stated, "As long as I'm alive, and as long as I'm rich, the New Beverly will be there, showing double features in 35mm."

BEST TIME TO GO: It usually only shows one double feature a night, and they tend to sell out, so get your tickets online and line up early.
PARKING: Metered street parking, but the adjacent neighborhood is permit only, so be careful.

Pantages Theater

6233 Hollywood Boulevard, Los Angeles, CA 90028

Hollywood venue for live theater and music.

When Broadway comes to Hollywood, it usually come to the Pantages. The theater opened as a stop on the vaudeville circuit in 1930, but the Great Depression forced it to cut costs; it primarily became a movie house for the next several decades. The second floor later held the personal offices of Howard Hughes, and the Academy Awards were held at the venue from 1949 to 1959. The '70s saw a return to large-scale live theater performances, and the Pantages has since played host to sold-out runs of *The Lion King*, *Hamilton* and *Wicked*. It's a great place to catch a concert too.

BEST TIME TO GO: There are shows most nights, but the ornate façade is worth a look in and of itself.
PARKING: It's Hollywood, so look for something on the street first and then head for a pay lot.

Walt Disney Concert Hall

111 South Grand Avenue, Los Angeles, CA 90012

Acoustically flawless complex for classical music.

Frank Gehry and his ambitious, abstract building designs have made him one of the most in-demand architects in Los Angeles for high-profile, public-facing projects. One of his best-known projects is the Walt Disney Concert Hall. No, it has nothing to do with Disneyland; it is instead a "gift" to the people of Los Angeles from the Disney family. While Gehry was the primary architect for the building, the acoustic elements were designed by Minoru Nagata and have been praised for their precision. The hall is primarily used as a venue for the Los Angeles Philharmonic, but it has a vast array of performances and sometimes even rock concerts. Many come just to enjoy the swooping, angular design of the building. The stainless steel façade has become a popular photo op for tourists but has not been without controversy. Originally, the glare from Disney Concert Hall caused adjacent buildings to heat up and caused hot spots of

Right: The Pantages Theater is a popular venue for touring stage productions. *Carol Highsmith.*

Below: Walt Disney Concert Hall was designed by architect Frank Gehry. *Carol Highsmith.*

more than 140 degrees on the sidewalks and even a few traffic accidents. Gehry and his team were brought back in to sand down and dull the offending panels.

BEST TIME TO GO: The grounds are open during the day to hang out in. It's a nice stop if you're in the area to see MOCA or the Broad.
PARKING: This part of downtown is difficult to find cheap and easy parking. The garage beneath the concert hall cost LA County $110 million so maybe just use that.

Hollywood Bowl

2301 North Highland Avenue, Los Angeles, CA 90068

Historic outdoor concert venue and summer staple.

The Hollywood Bowl is one of the premier concert venues in Los Angeles and is considered one of the best live music venues in America. The Bowl officially opened on July 11, 1922, and through the years has hosted everything from Easter service to Doors concerts. The Beatles played here twice, in 1964 and 1965. During the summer, the Bowl is the home to the Los Angeles Philharmonic. It's very popular with locals for its policy of allowing visitors to bring in their own food and alcohol on select nights. Randy Newman performed here once, and when the whole audience sang along to "I Love L.A." under the stars, it was truly magical.

BEST TIME TO GO: Events booked by the Bowl themselves are BYOB. "Leased Events" are not.
PARKING: Parking is always a nightmare no matter what. Best bet is to park near Hollywood Boulevard and walk up.

The Troubadour

9081 North Santa Monica Boulevard, West Hollywood, CA 90069

Small club great for catching up-and-comers.

After the excitement from the psychedelic heyday of the mid-'60s Sunset Strip began to fade, the action moved a little down the road to Santa Monica and Doheny and owner Doug Weston's Troubadour Club. The Troubadour opened as a folk club in the late 1950s and gradually became a hub for the emerging singer-songwriter movement a decade later. Many musicians who would become household names got their start at the club, including James Taylor, Carole King, Jackson Browne and Elton John, whose star-making first U.S. show was at the Troubadour. The club gained a reputation as a place to see top-notch talent in an intimate setting—not because they liked playing there necessarily, but because the enterprising Weston would sign new acts to onerous booking contracts requiring them to play the club long after they had outgrown it. The Troubadour is no longer the hottest club in town but miraculously has been able to keep its doors open continuously booking live music most nights of the week.

BEST TIME TO GO: Occasionally some big names or old-timers will do special shows here, but the booking is very eclectic so check the calendar well in advance.

PARKING: There are meters around. Farther south on Doheny, you can usually find free parking and then walk up.

Whiskey a Go Go

8901 Sunset Boulevard, West Hollywood, CA 90069

Legendary club, a shell of its former self, still kicking.

The Whiskey is one the worst places to see live music. The drinks are expensive, the sound is bad and it's horrendously decorated. But that's not how it used to be. Back in the '60s, this was the spot. The club opened in 1964 with Johnny "Secret Agent Man" Rivers as the star attraction. Rivers's

The Whiskey a Go Go was host to many up-and-coming bands but has been reduced to a pay-to-play business model. *Adam Papagan.*

performances were supplemented by women in short dresses and white boots dancing in cages suspended from the ceiling, kick-starting the go-go craze. Before long, the Whiskey became the epicenter for LA's blossoming rock scene, with bands like the Doors, the Byrds, Love and Buffalo Springfield all performing there regularly. A fire in the early '70s destroyed much of the original interior, and the action moved elsewhere. The club had a resurgence in the 1980s hosting punk and metal shows, but it was never quite the same. Today, the club is strictly pay-to-play, meaning acts are charged by the venue for the right to perform. It's unlikely you'll see your favorite band play there, but on the right night, you can look up at the stage that hosted so many of the greats and still feel that last bit of nostalgia.

BEST TIME TO GO: It's pretty dismal there, but check the calendar and maybe you'll get lucky.
PARKING: As with every place on the Sunset Strip, start by looking for a meter then submit to a paid parking lot.

Roxy Theater

9009 Sunset Boulevard, West Hollywood, CA 90069

Sunset Strip club that has hosted many major artists.

There's a lot of history in the little Roxy Theater. The club was opened in 1973 by some of the same names behind the smaller Whiskey a Go Go down the street. This is the location of the American premiere of *The Rocky Horror Show*, prior to it being turned into a movie. Pretty much everyone has played here at one point or another. It is the recording location of numerous live albums, including those by Bob Marley, Frank Zappa, Van Morrison, Bruce Springsteen, Neil Young, Warren Zevon and Richard Pryor.

My favorite story about the Roxy is from when Nirvana played there in 1991. The band was all set to release their landmark album *Nevermind* and scheduled a showcase for fans and music executives. Their label, Geffen, had just released the double Guns N' Roses album *Use Your Illusion* but, after seeing Nirvana perform, decided to shift its promotional efforts on breaking *Nevermind* into the mainstream, launching Nirvana into unfathomable success and kick-starting the grunge movement. It was a watershed moment in music history, but just another night at the Roxy.

Numerous live albums were recorded at the Roxy. *Adam Papagan.*

BEST TIME TO GO: Shows most nights of the week.
PARKING: This is a typical Sunset Strip parking situation. If you just want a picture, it's easy to pull over. If you're going to a show, you'll likely be there longer than the parking meter allows, so you may just have to bite the bullet on valet parking.

The Viper Room

8852 Sunset Boulevard, West Hollywood, CA 90069

One-time celebrity hotspot anticipating a new life.

The Viper Room is one of the last remaining rock clubs on the once-frenetic Sunset Strip. In the 1990s, it was known as a hip hangout for young Hollywood types, particularly because actor Johnny Depp was part owner. Back in the day, many high-profile performers like Tom Petty and Johnny Cash would do small shows at the club for lucky and in-the-know patrons. Celebrity tragedy aficionados may also know the Viper Room as the site of young actor River Phoenix's fatal drug overdose. Depp has long since relinquished his ownership, and the club has devolved into another pay-to-play venue. The whole block is currently slated for eventual demolition to make way for yet another boutique hotel. The new development will, however, include a small museum and music venue that will bear the iconic club's name.

BEST TIME TO GO: It's booking less and less music these days, so check before you go.
PARKING: It's the Sunset Strip, so basically impossible to find easy parking. You can look for a meter, but beware of the permitted residential streets.

Vibrato Grill Jazz

2930 Beverly Glen Circle, Los Angeles, CA 90077

Swanky nightclub hidden in a hilltop shopping center.

Tucked discreetly into the corner of a strip mall in the hills between Beverly Hills and Bel Air is Herb Alpert's Vibrato Grill Jazz. Alpert is, of course, the "A" in A&M Records and the trumpeter responsible for all of those busy, horn-driven Tijuana Brass albums of the 1960s. Despite how corny the Tijuana Brass was, Vibrato is actually a very hip scene. The restaurant features live music every night of the week and a pretty good menu to accompany it. There's usually always a cover and item minimum, so it's not a cheap night out, but stepping through the doors brings you into a world where stylish elites sip martinis, nibble on steaks and listen to top-notch jazz. The restaurant is also decorated with Alpert's visual art, which probably wouldn't have made the cut had he not been the owner of the restaurant.

BEST TIME TO GO: Every time I've been here, it's been popping.
PARKING: It has valet but also free parking in the same lot.

The Comedy Store

8433 Sunset Boulevard, Los Angeles, CA 90069

Haunted comedy club with big name drop-ins.

The Comedy Store is the grimiest and most realistic of Hollywood's major comedy clubs. The dreams of the thousands of aspiring performers who have passed through the Comedy Store's doors are literally soaked into the club's stained carpet. The venue was opened by comedian Sammy Shore in 1972 and subsequently lost to his wife, Mitzi, in their divorce the following year. Countless performers—including Robin Williams, Jay Leno, Richard Pryor and Sam Kinison—developed their careers here. Many of the names of the club's regulars are painted on the outside of the building. Shore was a notoriously tough woman to work for and, for years, had a "no pay policy" for comedians, arguing that the exposure the club gave to new talent was compensation enough. This resulted in a labor strike in the late '70s that was eventually won by the comedians. After the strike, certain performers were no longer allowed to work at the club, like Steve Lubetkin, who committed suicide by jumping off the roof of the hotel next door with a note reading, "My name is Steve Lubetkin, and I used to work at The Comedy Store." Today, it does pay the comedians, and it is still a showcase for up-and-coming talent and established veterans working out new material.

BEST TIME TO GO: Weeknights are your best bet to catch a big name doing a drop-in. They're usually on the road on weekends.
PARKING: Nearly impossible on the Sunset Strip, but there is a public pay lot just west of La Cienega near the Store.

The Laugh Factory

8001 Sunset Boulevard, Los Angeles, CA 90046

Sunset Strip comedy club and site of past controversy.

The Laugh Factory has been one of LA's major comedy clubs since opening on Sunset Boulevard in 1979. It's pretty typical for a Los Angeles club, and on any given night, you're likely to see an entertaining mixture of up-and-comers, established comics and has-beens working out new material to take on the road. The club is located between Hollywood Boulevard and the Sunset Strip, so it's one that I drive by a lot while giving tours. Guests are typically unfamiliar with the Laugh Factory until I mention that this is where Michael Richards, aka Kramer from *Seinfeld*, yelled the n-word repeatedly on stage in 2006.

BEST TIME TO GO: You're likely to see big names on weeknights.
PARKING: Valet, or you might be able to find street parking a little farther east.

SoFi Stadium

1001 Stadium Drive, Inglewood, CA 90301

Modern venue for top sports and entertainment events.

Although it's one of LA's newest mega venues, SoFi Stadium has already been home to two NFL teams, a Super Bowl and performances from BTS, Paul McCartney, Taylor Swift, Beyoncé and the Rolling Stones. The sleek stadium holds an average of seventy thousand guests per event, making it one of the largest venues of its kind anywhere. The next few years will also see World Cup matches and Wrestlemania visiting SoFi. There's a card casino at the southern end of the development, so there really is something for every taste here.

BEST TIME TO GO: Try to get here soon while everything is still shiny and new. With hundreds of thousands of visitors in a given week, it's bound to get trashed sooner or later.

PARKING: It's a trek, but there's free street parking on Crenshaw south of Manchester. Otherwise, be prepared to pay some of the most expensive parking rates around.

Dodger Stadium

1000 Vin Scully Avenue, Los Angeles, CA 90012

The world's largest ballpark.

Dodger Stadium is actually the third-oldest ballpark in the United States, behind only Fenway Park and Wrigley Field. So why hasn't the stadium been knocked down yet in favor of a newer, shinier one? The answer is the enormous number of fans it can accommodate. With fifty-six thousand seats, it is the largest ballpark by seating capacity in the world. Construction on the stadium began in the late '50s in what was once the largely Hispanic neighborhood of Chavez Ravine. The land had originally been acquired via eminent domain to build a public housing project, but voters overwhelmingly approved a referendum to build a baseball stadium there instead. Many families were displaced, but the stadium rose from the canyon. Besides being home to the Dodgers, the stadium is also notable for being the location of

Dodger Stadium has more seats than any other ballpark in the world. *Carol Highsmith.*

one of the Beatles' final concerts and a Mass given by Pope John Paul II during his visit in 1987.

BEST TIME TO GO: The summer sun in LA can get hot, so I've always preferred night games.
PARKING: Because of the location, you pretty much have to pay to park there. You may be able to find something on the streets of Elysian Park, but it's a long walk. There's also a bus that runs from Union Station.

Crypto.com Arena

1111 South Figueroa Street, Los Angeles, CA 90015

Pro sports complex in the heart of downtown.

Formerly Staples Center, the "House that Kobe Built" is home to the Lakers, the Clippers, the Sparks and the Kings and welcomes more than 4 million guests annually. Star Plaza outside honors LA sports legends like Magic Johnson and Wayne Gretzky with statues of the famous athletes. The venue is also the frequent venue for the Grammy Awards and was also the location

Staples Center was renamed Crypto.com Arena in 2021. *Carol Highsmith.*

of Michael Jackson's memorial service. When the name was changed in 2021, a lot of people were upset. I was surprised Staples had such a loyal fan base.

BEST TIME TO GO: During a game or concert. Don't waste your time at the dismal LA Live complex surrounding the arena.

PARKING: Parking at sporting events is always overpriced. There is some free street parking about a mile west of the arena, but it's maybe an hour walk until you actually get to your seats.

Chapter 8

DINING AND SHOPPING

By now, we've been all over LA, and you're probably getting hungry. LA's food scene is as diverse and contradictory as anything else here. Many people associate Los Angeles with ultra-healthy vegetarian eating, but we're also the birthplace of the fast-food culture that has infiltrated the entire country. We have "chef driven" fine dining, but also mind-blowingly flavorful international cuisine proliferating our many immigrant communities. There's just too many great restaurants to name here, so instead we'll focus on the ones that give LA a unique sense of place. Ultimately, LA has a lot of different kinds of people, so we have a lot of different kinds of places to eat. After your meal we've curated some shopping options for other unique and interesting ways to spend your money.

Norms

Various locations

Vintage spot for a good old-fashioned meal.

There are a million greasy spoon–style diners across America. So what makes Norms special? Well, nothing in particular, which is what makes it significant. In the ever-changing landscape of Los Angeles, Norms has been there twenty-four hours a day, seven days a week, serving up simple, hearty, cheap food. Everyone eats at Norms—old, young, famous, average, rich and

The La Cienega location of Norms Restaurant opened in 1957. *Adam Papagan.*

working class—basically any type of person you can find in Los Angeles. The Googie-style architecture of the flagship La Cienega location puts you simultaneously in the past, present and future. This isn't a bucket list place to visit, but if you're looking for a true SoCal food experience, grab a seat at the counter at Norms.

BEST TIME TO GO: Open twenty-four hours.
PARKING: Parking lot.

The Original Farmers Market

6333 West 3rd Street, Los Angeles, CA 90036

Food court for vintage local eateries.

The Farmers Market and its old-timey food court is the best place to stop off for lunch when touring around Los Angeles. Unlike most farmers' markets, which pop up only once or twice a week, the Original Farmers Market of Los Angeles is a permanent installation open seven days a week. Most of the restaurants are independent or family-owned and have been in operation for decades. Some even date back to the market's opening in the 1930s. There's something for every palate here—Chinese, tacos, barbecue, Cajun—so if there's a specific cuisine you're looking to try while in town, they'll probably have it. It's not uncommon to see intrepid international tourists enjoying their first hamburger with a fork and knife. Adjoining the market is the over-the-top Vegas meets Disneyland-style mall, the Grove, which is worth a stop for some post-digestion shopping.

BEST TIME TO GO: Lunch. Most restaurants close before 8:00 p.m.
PARKING: There's a parking lot. Tour guides park for free.

Donuts

Various locations

One of SoCal's most iconic foods.

The main foods Southern California is known for are tacos, burgers and donuts. Late-night tacos can be found on nearly every corner if you know where to look and are always delicious. Our place in fast-food history is secure, being the birthplace of McDonald's, Del Taco, In-N-Out and Jack in the Box. For donuts, you have to be a little more in the know. There's Randy's Donuts by the airport, known for the enormous donut on the roof. California Donuts is popular for its unique toppings like Lucky Charms and bacon. Out in the suburbs is the Donut Hole in La Puente, where you actually get to drive through a giant concrete donut to pick up your order. And, of course, there is the Donut Man at Grand Central Market, famous locally for his fresh strawberry donuts. Nevertheless, you can't go wrong visiting one of the hundreds of mom and pop donut shops across the Southland. Get a cup of coffee, too, for dunking.

BEST TIME TO GO: Most donut shops have long hours, so they make a great snack any time of day.
PARKING: Almost always in a strip mall.

Oldest Operating McDonald's

10207 Lakewood Boulevard, Downey, CA 90240

Pilgrimage site for fans of fast-food history.

Just south of Los Angeles in the beautiful city of Downey is one of the most significant pieces of commercial architecture in all of America: the world's oldest operating McDonald's restaurant. This is not the first McDonald's (the original location opened by the McDonald brothers in San Bernardino was demolished ages ago), nor is it the official birthplace of McDonald's (that honor goes to Ray Kroc's first franchise in Des Plaines, Illinois), but this is the third built overall and the oldest one still standing. Since this location predates Kroc's involvement with the company, it was for decades the only independent franchise in the chain, saving it from corporate-ordered modernization and refurbishment. The building sports the original, iconic Golden Arches design, as well as a larger-than-life sign featuring Speedee, the company's first mascot. The restaurant was officially acquired by the McDonald's Corporation in 1990 and updated with a drive-thru and adjacent restroom/museums featuring artifacts, an informational video and a very creepy Mac Tonight costume. For better or worse, millions of people around the world eat McDonald's hamburgers every day, and it all started in Southern California.

BEST TIME TO GO: I always stop here on my way down to Disneyland.
PARKING: Parking lot.

Left: The lobby of the Hollywood Roosevelt was renovated in 2005. *Adam Papagan.*

Below: Olvera Street, Los Angeles' oldest street, mixes history and kitsch. *Carol Highsmith.*

Left: Doors frontman and "27 Club" member Jim Morrison is still a recognizable figure in Los Angeles. Here an electrical box has been vandalized with his image near his home in Laurel Canyon. *Adam Papagan*.

Below: The Venice Boardwalk is known for its unique vendors and vibrant street entertainers. *Carol Highsmith.*

Opposite, top: Los Angeles' Chinatown was fancifully designed to attract tourists. *Adam Papagan.*

Opposite, bottom: Crossroads of the World was one of the original outdoor shopping centers, a form that now proliferates throughout Southern California. *Adam Papagan.*

CROSSRO DS
6671 OF THE WORLD

Left: Angels Flight has operated intermittently since 1901. *Adam Papagan.*

Below: The auditorium of Hollywood High School features a mural of famous alumni along with a few celebrities who did not attend the school. *Carol Highsmith.*

Right: The opulent Beverly Hills City Hall was built during the height of the Great Depression. *Carol Highsmith.*

Below: Union Station remains a bustling transportation hub. *Carol Highsmith.*

Top: The original residents of the ultra-swanky Stahl House were a middle-class Los Angeles family. *Adam Papagan.*

Bottom: The Frederick R. Weisman Art Foundation features work from many well-known twentieth-century artists. *Adam Papagan.*

Right: Culver City's Bhagavad-gita Museum is operated by the International Society of Krishna Consciousness. *Adam Papagan.*

Below: The Beverly Hills Hotel, depicted on this illustrated postcard, would later be featured on the cover of the Eagles album *Hotel California*. *Detroit Publishing Company.*

Above: The original gates of the Fox Studio are now surrounded by a residential neighborhood. *Adam Papagan.*

Left: The Sony Pictures lot is the former home of MGM, where *The Wizard of Oz* was filmed. *Adam Papagan.*

Opposite, top: Canter's Deli is a beloved twenty-four-hour Hollywood institution. *Adam Papagan.*

Opposite, bottom: Opening hours are the best time to avoid lines at Pink's Hot Dogs. *Adam Papagan.*

Canters
RESTAURANT
BAKERY
DELICATESSEN

MADE SPECIAL FOR
PINK'S
DOGS
PINK'S
SINCE 1939

Frolic
Room
Cocktails

Opposite, top: Motörhead's Lemmy Kilmister was a regular at the Rainbow Bar and Grill and is honored with a life-size statue. *Adam Papagan.*

Opposite, bottom: Dive bars and celebrity impersonators are two common sights on Hollywood Boulevard. *Carol Highsmith.*

Above: The hotel room where Janis Joplin died is only one block from the Chinese Theater. *Adam Papagan.*

Right: The Bunny Museum is home to thousands of bunny artifacts and ephemera. *Adam Papagan*

Left: Los Angeles is one of the few places in the world where asphalt lakes, or tar pits, occur. *Carol Highsmith.*

Below: The stretch of the Pacific Coast Highway that runs through Malibu has been the location of many celebrity scandals and misadventures. *Carol Highsmith.*

Above: The Compton Drive-In offers a less gritty depiction of the city than how the area is often portrayed in the media. *John Margolis.*

Right: Bakers across Los Angeles use donut-shaped signage to attract customers. *John Margolis*

Segments of the Berlin Wall reassembled on Wilshire Boulevard. *Adam Papagan.*

Developer Abbot Kinney modeled his town after Venice, Italy. *Library of Congress.*

Above: The Brown Derby restaurant on Wilshire was the only location actually shaped like a hat. *John Margolis.*

Left: The Beverly Hills Hotel is one place you are reliably likely to see a celebrity. *Adam Papagan.*

Top: Capitol Records is an instantly recognizable feature of the Los Angeles skyline. *Carol Highsmith.*

Bottom: Grauman's Chinese is Hollywood's quintessential theater. *Adam Papagan.*

In-N-Out

Various locations

SoCal's quintessential hamburger experience.

Want to eat like a local? In-N-Out is a beloved regional burger chain that's become famous around the world for its inexpensive and highly delicious burgers. The restaurant chain was founded in 1948 in the Los Angeles suburb of Baldwin Park, and the company is still headquartered in basically the same location today. It's still family-owned, and there's a strict emphasis on quality, both in terms of food and management. The menu is simple: just burgers, fries, soda and shakes, but locals tend to order from the "secret menu," preferring their burgers "Animal Style." Many East Coasters find the hype underwhelming, but this is as quintessential Southern California as it gets.

BEST TIME TO GO: There's always a line, so be prepared to be there a while. The restaurant should really just be called "In." Counter service is generally quicker than the drive-thru.

PARKING: Most locations have a parking lot or at least a drive-thru.

In-N-Out is known for its simple and affordable menu. *Carol Highsmith.*

Canter's Deli

417 North Fairfax Avenue, Los Angeles, CA 90036

A rocking, all-night deli.

Due to its late hours and proximity to the Sunset Strip, this 24/7 deli has long been a hangout for rock stars, celebrities and counterculture types. Owner Marc Canter is a childhood friend of Slash from the band Guns N' Roses, and a back booth served as the group's hangout during the band's early days. The adjoining Kibitz Room features live music (usually to complaints from the waitresses) and is one of the last true dive bars in the area. LA may have other delis and LA may have better delis, but none is quite like Canter's.

BEST TIME TO GO: Open twenty-four hours. At night, it's quite the scene.
PARKING: It has its own lot, which is invaluable on Fairfax.

Celebrity Hotspot Restaurants

Various locations around the Westside

Grazing grounds for the rich and famous.

For how big and diverse Los Angeles is, it always seems that the elites prefer to gather in the same few areas and hang with the same few people. Because of this, there are always a few reliable hangouts where celebrities go to eat, drink and either avoid the paparazzi or be seen by them. So many have come and gone over the years—the Brown Derby, the Daisy, Spago, Dan Tana's, the Ivy, Nobu, the Palm, Craig's and more. As a rule, they are usually crowded, small and overpriced, and the food is hit or miss. If this is your sort of thing, I recommend checking TMZ or Page Six to see what the hot restaurant of the moment is. It can be exciting to see a celebrity grazing in the wild, but be warned that approaching one while eating is strictly discouraged. Locals know that all the best restaurants in LA are in strip malls anyway.

BEST TIME TO GO: Dinner.
PARKING: Valet. Always valet.

Tail o' the Pup

8512 Santa Monica Boulevard, West Hollywood, CA 90069

A hot dog stand shaped like a hot dog.

It's hard not to love a building shaped like the thing it sells. For decades, Tail o' the Pup, a hot dog stand in the shape of a giant hot dog, was one of Los Angeles' most recognizable landmarks, right up there with the Chinese Theater and the Hollywood Sign. It was a familiar sight in commercials, music videos, movies and any other project trying to convey the wackiness of Los Angeles. Then, suddenly in 2005, the hot dog building disappeared. Rumors circulated among locals that it might be stashed away in a storage container or in the hands of a private collector. A decade later, it turned up in the storage yard of the Valley Relics Museum. The Valley Relics people eventually got it into the hands of restaurant developers the 1933 Group, which painstakingly restored and updated the beloved building and moved it to its current home on Santa Monica Boulevard. Now it's back for new generations to enjoy and already a hotspot for social media selfies. It's a happy ending to the Tail o' the Pup tale.

This is a double landmark, as the new building that holds the hot dog was once the practice space for the band the Doors. Their album *L.A. Woman* was recorded here, and there's a picture of Jim Morrison near the vocal booth/bathroom.

BEST TIME TO GO: The outdoor seating makes it a great lunch spot.
PARKING: It doesn't have a parking lot, but there are a few meters nearby.

Pink's Hot Dogs

709 North La Brea Avenue, Los Angeles, CA 90038

Hot dog stand known for long lines and famous patrons.

There's an urban legend that Orson Welles used to pull his limousine up to Pink's and have tray after tray of chili dogs brought out to the car. This is probably not true, but it speaks to Pink's status as the favorite celebrity hot dog. The restaurant, begun as a simple push cart in 1939, has been serving the Hollywood community from the very beginning. The menu features many specialty items named after its famous patrons like Martha Stewart,

Rosie O'Donnell, Carl Reiner and Ed Asner, among others. Pink's is very proud of its celebrity clientele, and the dining room is decorated floor to ceiling with autographed headshots. Apart from the hype, they really are good hot dogs, and plenty of regular people enjoy them too.

BEST TIME TO GO: I love going in the morning right when it opens. It's not a traditional breakfast, but there's no line.
PARKING: There's have a lot. Enter on La Brea.

Grand Central Market

317 South Broadway, Los Angeles, CA 90013

Eclectic downtown food hall.

Grand Central Market is LA's oldest and largest public market. Its building, built in 1917, was Los Angeles' first steel-framed, fireproof structure. The market features more than forty restaurants and food vendors, many with dazzling neon signs. Its tenants are a mixture of legacy businesses and cutting-edge foodie destinations. It's the ideal spot for lunch if you're visiting the Bradbury Building, Angels Flight or other downtown landmarks.

BEST TIME TO GO: Lunch.
PARKING: There are numerous pay-by-the-hour lots in the area.

Grand Central Market is a go-to lunch spot for tourists and downtown office workers alike. *Carol Highsmith.*

Rainbow Bar and Grill

9015 Sunset Boulevard, West Hollywood, CA 90069

An '80s rock-and-roll time warp with pretty good food.

The Rainbow Bar and Grill is like the Hard Rock Café but real. Yes, like Hard Rock, there are gold records and guitars on the walls, but this is an actual rock star hangout that musicians have been frequenting since the '70s. John Lennon and his drinking buddies, the Hollywood Vampires, used to hold court in the VIP section. You can sit in the exact spot where John probably snorted cocaine. Lemmy from Motörhead, also a regular, allegedly moved to an apartment a few blocks away specifically because of its proximity to the Rainbow. The food is surprisingly great too. Ozzy Osbourne has proclaimed the restaurant has the "best pizza in the world." The aesthetic hasn't moved much past the 1980s hair metal heyday, but this is a must-stop pilgrimage for all rockers visiting Los Angeles.

BEST TIME TO GO: It serves food late. I love getting a big plate of tortellini in the middle of the night.

PARKING: You might be able to find a meter on Sunset, but they also have valet parking (very rock-and-roll!).

Musso & Frank

6667 Hollywood Boulevard, Hollywood, CA 90028

Classic Hollywood eatery for stars and tourists.

Musso & Frank is quintessential Old Hollywood. In fact, Musso's is the oldest restaurant in Hollywood and hasn't really changed much since opening in 1919. The booths and wallpaper look the same, the (mostly male) waitstaff still wear their signature red tuxedo jackets and the menu still boasts many long-forgotten dishes like Welsh rarebit and lobster Thermidor, which most restaurants removed from their menus decades ago. Of course, the restaurant has been a hub for the movie industry and creative folks from the beginning. Charlie Chaplin dined here, naturally, as did Wyatt Earp, a real cowboy who spent his twilight years playing one in the movies. Although the restaurant's popularity has ebbed and flowed over the years, a recent appearance in Quentin Tarantino's *Once Upon a Time...in Hollywood* has given Musso's a renewed popularity with the hip crowd, and you can find Hollywood's newest generation of sophisticates sidled up to the bar enjoying a gin fizz.

BEST TIME TO GO: I like grabbing a seat at the bar right when it opens at the beginning of a night out on Hollywood Boulevard.
PARKING: Valet.

Yamashiro

1999 North Sycamore Avenue, Los Angeles, CA 90068

Palatial hillside restaurant for sushi and drinks.

Yamashiro means "mountain castle" in Japanese. The elegant restaurant was built originally as a house modeled after real buildings in Japan for a pair of German American brothers to hold their vast collection of Japanese antiques. It was one of the first truly grand homes in Hollywood. Elites flocked to the property as a private club in the 1920s, but the Great Depression put pressure on the brothers' finances, forcing them to open the house to the public for tours. Yamashiro kept a low profile during the anti-Japanese sentiment of World War II. By the 1950s, things began to cool off, and it opened as a proper restaurant and extensive Japanese garden. It's closed and reopened multiple times over the years, but its prime hillside location makes it a Hollywood staple.

BEST TIME TO GO: The food is good but pricey, so this is a good place to go for drinks around sundown.
PARKING: You can park for free at the bottom of the hill and walk up, but you'll look like a schlub. Best to take advantage of the valet parking.

The Frolic Room

6245 Hollywood Boulevard, Los Angeles, CA 90028

Cheap film noir dive bar.

And the award for Best Dive Bar goes to.… Located at the famous intersection of Hollywood and Vine, the Frolic Room opened initially as an illegal speakeasy, then legally in 1934, just after the end of Prohibition. Its dingy atmosphere and neon sign, which haven't changed since its opening, are like something out of an old detective novel. The patrons are just about every type of person you can find in Hollywood—locals, tourists, the famous and the infamous. Every Oscar Sunday, the bar shows the award ceremony on its small TV. It's fun to watch it with the regulars while the actual awards are happening just down the street.

BEST TIME TO GO: Despite its size, it's never that crowded. For some reason, I always find myself here during the day.
PARKING: Metered parking off Hollywood.

Rodeo Drive

Beverly Hills between Santa Monica and Wilshire

Three block shopping district known for expensive stores.

Rodeo Drive is billed as the most famous and luxurious shopping street on the planet. In reality, the three-block stretch in Beverly Hills' central business district is occupied mainly by big luxury brands you can find in any major city. It's nice stuff, to be sure—Gucci, Louis Vuitton, Dior, Rolex. It's also a

Due to its high concentration of luxury fashion brands, Rodeo Drive is often referred to as the most expensive street in the world. *Carol Highsmith.*

popular place for people to show off their (rented) luxury cars. It's very likely that you'll be sitting in traffic next to a Ferrari or Lamborghini at some point on your visit. Get out for a few minutes, however, and you'll notice there are a lot of people milling about but not a lot of shopping bags. Many of the stores on Rodeo operate at a loss simply to be associated with the famous street. One block over on Canon Drive, there are regular stores like Pottery Barn and Sephora.

BEST TIME TO GO: Things don't really get rolling over there until after 11:00 a.m.
PARKING: The residential area north of Santa Monica Boulevard has free two-hour parking.

The Grove

189 The Grove Drive, Los Angeles, CA 90036

Carefully controlled shopping fantasyland.

The Grove is sort of like Disneyland without the rides or the magic—and if it was just a mall. The shopping center immediately next to the Original Farmers Market opened in 2002 and is themed to resemble a familiar (small-town America? Europe?) yet whimsical streetscape complete with curbs, streetlamps and a functioning trolley car running through the middle. The stores are ones you'd find in pretty much any mall—Nordstrom, Cheesecake Factory, Nike—but here they are presented as essential landmarks fashioned around the Grove's faux town square. It's kind of like Las Vegas but without any of the fun stuff. The mall was developed by millionaire Rick Caruso, a somewhat controversial figure who switched his political affiliation to Democrat days before announcing his candidacy for Los Angeles mayor. Many feared that if elected, Caruso would turn the whole city into an extended version of the Grove. Caruso inevitably lost his bid for mayor, and today, people of all political associations still happily pose in front of the Grove's dancing fountain.

BEST TIME TO GO: If you happen to be in town around Christmas, it has a fake snowfall every night.
PARKING: There's a big parking structure and not many other alternatives. Millionaire Caruso charges mall employees to park there.

Citadel Outlets

100 Citadel Drive, Commerce, CA 90040

Fantastical shopping center for international deal hunters.

The building that houses the Citadel Outlets was once a tire factory. *Adam Papagan.*

Outlet malls can be a big draw for international tourists. In some countries, luxury items are heavily taxed, and travelers will plan entire vacations around a visit to the outlet mall. Many of the stores carry items not nice or fashionable enough to sell in regular stores, but the opportunity to participate in good old American consumerism is an allure in itself. The Citadel Outlets, located just southeast of Downtown LA in the liminal City of Commerce, are hard to miss from the freeway. The site is an adaptive redevelopment of the old Samson Tire and Rubber Company building, which was built in 1929 in the inexplicable style of the castle of Assyrian king Sargon II. Vintage stonework with depictions of ancient legends are nestled in between outlets for companies like Uggs and Calvin Klein, making whole place like a temple to buying slightly discounted items.

I was once hired for a custom private tour by two Indonesian businessmen. All they wanted to do was visit the outside of Warner Bros. to get a picture, the outside of Universal Studios to get a picture and then spend three hours at Citadel Outlets. Luckily for me, I was left to explore the exotic architecture while they shopped. When they were done, we had a few more hours until I had to take them to the airport, and I asked if there was anything else they wanted to see. The only other thing they could think of was LAPD headquarters. This wasn't a typical tour, but it proves that there are many competing, equally valid interpretations of what Los Angeles represents to the world.

BEST TIME TO GO: Less crowded on weekdays.
PARKING: Parking lot.

It's a Wrap

3315 Magnolia Boulevard, Burbank, CA 91505

Resale shop for secondhand wardrobe.

Ever watch an episode of *The Young and the Restless* and think, "Man, I wish I could dress like that guy"? There's a store in Burbank that has you covered. It's a Wrap is a secondhand clothing store that exclusively resells used props and wardrobes from movies and TV shows. When a show gets canceled or a production company is looking to thin out its excess wardrobe, they call It's a Wrap to come pick it up and resell it to the general public at rock-bottom prices. Located just down the street from many of the major studios, the store mainly carries contemporary clothes like you would find at a major department store, although you will find the odd vintage item or period costume. Each piece is tagged with a special code stating what production it was used in. Some of the best costumes are held over for Halloween and go on sale in mid-September. A lot of the clothes aren't exactly trendy, but the thrill of the hunt is what attracts most people. If you're looking for unique souvenir items, here are some you can wear back home with you.

BEST TIME TO GO: Receives new stock daily.
PARKING: Street parking on Magnolia.

Larry Edmunds Bookshop

6644 Hollywood Boulevard, Los Angeles, CA 90028

Books about movies.

Back in the day, Hollywood Boulevard was almost as well known for its concentration of bookstores as it was for its movie theaters. The Boulevard has changed a lot over the years, and the only bookstore left is Larry Edmunds. The store opened in the late '30s and, in its first iteration, mainly sold rare books, first editions, imports and erotica to writers and studio execs. After the war, the store shifted to specializing in books about the film industry itself, and today it is the go-to spot for scripts, photographs, posters, biographies and anything entertainment-related. The store is a treasured resource for film buffs. Quentin Tarantino even re-created the original signage as a set piece for his film *Once Upon a Time…in Hollywood*.

BEST TIME TO GO: It's a nice addendum to a trip to Hollywood Boulevard.
PARKING: There are almost always meters by the store just off Hollywood Boulevard.

The Last Bookstore

453 South Spring Street, ground floor, Los Angeles, CA 90013

Photo-friendly shop for literature and records.

Reports of the brick-and-mortar bookstore's demise have been highly exaggerated. Although the Last Bookstore is (thankfully) far from the only good used bookstore in Los Angeles, it may just be the last bookstore you'll ever need. The store got into Downtown LA at just the right time, and as the neighborhood has been revitalized, the Last Bookstore has blossomed into one of the largest used booksellers in the country. This is another one in the "something for everyone" category. There are new and used books, yes, but also departments for comics and records (more my thing). There's also an annex for rare books and unique items, which you should hit first if your browsing time is limited. Social media users may recognize the store's "book tunnel" installation, which is perfect for letting your followers know that you're not just in LA to see celebrities—you are also quite cultured and well-read too.

BEST TIME TO GO: Downtown is weird because you never know what's going to be crowded and when, but it's usually not a chaotic shopping experience here.
PARKING: As with everything in downtown, look for a meter first before shelling out for a pay lot.

Amoeba Music

6200 Hollywood Boulevard, Los Angeles, CA 90028

The region's number one spot for physical media.

Any record store is worth a visit. You just never know what you're going to find. LA is full of them, but if you could only visit one, Amoeba is objectively the best record store in the county. There's something for everyone here

Amoeba Music's large selection caters to nearly every musical taste. *Adam Papagan.*

in every genre and format imaginable. It's not uncommon to see multiple generations of the same family loading up their shopping baskets together. In addition to music, the store also has an extensive inventory of used books, movies, posters, T-shirts and ephemera. Occasionally, it even hosts in-store concerts when a band puts out a new record. Over the years, the store has seen performances from Elvis Costello, Sharon Jones and The Dap Kings, Vampire Weekend, Joyce Manor, Belle and Sebastian and the Roots, all for free. Happy hunting!

BEST TIME TO GO: There are always people at Amoeba, so the atmosphere is fun. Even when it's crowded, the line moves quickly.
PARKING: There's a parking lot, and they validate with purchase, so if you're not buying anything else, just grab something from the dollar section. Otherwise, street parking can be tough in Hollywood.

Funko Hollywood

6201 Hollywood Boulevard #100, Los Angeles, CA 90028

Extra-large emporium for fashionable figurines.

The Funko Pop! Store could be easy to dismiss, but I actually think it's pretty cool. This is the flagship store of the pop culture collectible company, and they've really gone all out to cash in on the fad. Nearly life-size Funko Pop! figurines, with their large heads and vacant eyes, are elaborately staged in full immersive environments. All your favorites are here: Donald Duck, Thor, Harry Potter, Boba Fett and even advertising mascot Chester Cheeto. No intellectual property seems off limits. You can even have a custom Pop! made to look just like you. It's a little disappointing to see the characters depicted as Funkos and not how you're used to seeing them, but the lighting, music and sets are better than either of the wax museums down the street. The store is free to go to, but good luck getting out without buying anything.

BEST TIME TO GO: Lately, there's been a line to get in. It's definitely not worth waiting in the hot sun unless you're really into Funkos, but on a cool day, why not?
PARKING: You may have some luck with metered parking north of the store on Yucca.

Chapter 9

HAUNTED HORROR, SCANDAL AND TRUE CRIME

True crime locations are some of the most popular in LA. After all, Hollywood is nearly as well known for scandal and tragedy as it is for glitz and glamour. Everything here is filtered through a lens of entertainment, and people's biggest personal catastrophes become amusing cautionary tales. They are retold in the media again and again, making them legendary and mythical. Ironically, it is through death that these stories are given immortality and become an alluring connection to the past. Sometimes locations from movies about fictional tragedies become iconic in and of themselves, further blending the line between tragedy and entertainment. Here are some of the most haunted places and horrific events, both real and fake, that have happened in Los Angeles.

Forest Lawn

1712 South Glendale Avenue, Glendale, CA 91205

Odd, idyllic graveyard.

Forest Lawn Memorial Park is a cemetery concept so bizarre and macabre it could only have come out of Southern California. In 1917, Dr. Hubert Eaton had a vision to transform his cemetery from a place of sadness and gloom to a beautiful parklike setting reflecting the joyousness of life

The grave of controversial evangelist Aimee Semple McPherson. *Adam Papagan.*

after death. Flat grave markers were invented here so as to not distract from the impeccable landscaping. Elaborate marble statues were commissioned, and mausoleums were constructed in the style of famous European cathedrals. At Forest Lawn, you can find re-creations of all of Michelangelo's major works, an enormous rendering of *The Last Supper* in stained glass and artist Jan Styka's panoramic depiction of the Crucifixion, one of the largest paintings in the world. All of this is, of course completely incidental to Forest Lawn's core business of holding funerals and burying bodies. The juxtaposition is just as baffling as it is striking. Some believe that the cemetery's eclectic theming was an early influence on Walt Disney, who is also interred here. Speaking of which, a number of other celebrities have been laid to rest at Forest Lawn, including Clark Gable, W.C. Fields, Jean Harlow and Michael Jackson. Don't expect the cemetery staff to help you locate any of them, however. They're committed to keeping things tasteful.

BEST TIME TO GO: It closes at sundown. On weekdays, you're less likely to run into a funeral.
PARKING: Free. The grounds are huge, so you definitely need a car.

American Horror Story House

1120 Westchester Place, Los Angeles, CA 90019

Filming location for the popular anthology series.

The "Murder House" from *American Horror Story* is actually the real-life Rosenheim Mansion. Named for the architect who designed and built it in 1908, and declared an official historic landmark in 1999, the house has also been a filming location for other paranormal-themed shows like *Six Feet Under*, *The Twilight Zone* and *Dexter*. Most know it primarily as the setting of the first season of *AHS*, and fans still visit in steady numbers. Apparently, the house really is haunted—not by ghosts but by meddling tourists eager to get a selfie. In 2018, the current owners sued their real estate broker for not disclosing the house's connection to the series. They've since embraced the connection and occasionally host séances inside the house, which are live-streamed for twenty-five dollars. Private residence; please do not disturb occupants.

BEST TIME TO GO: There's never a bad time to go, but obviously, it's a little extra creepy at night.
PARKING: Ample street parking.

Michael Jackson's Death

100 North Carolwood Drive, Los Angeles, CA 90077

Location of one of the most shocking deaths of the twenty first century.

Michael Jackson's life was plagued by one scandal after another, but despite persistent and credible allegations of sexual abuse, he remains a hugely popular international celebrity years after his passing. Jackson was famous for most of his life. While his hits were a mainstay on the music charts, his bizarre personal life was a mainstay of the tabloids. This is the rented house Jackson was living in while rehearsing for comeback/farewell concert residency *This Is It*. While in a medically induced sleep, Jackson lost consciousness and was pronounced dead at Ronald Reagan Medical Center shortly after. The front gate the ambulance exits from in the famous TMZ video is largely unchanged. There are other important Jackson locations around Southern California—Neverland Ranch three hours north, his "hideout" on Wilshire Boulevard, the Jackson family compound in Encino—but this is where the sad story of the King of Pop comes to an end. Private residence; please do not disturb occupants.

BEST TIME TO GO: Anytime. During the day you'll see tour buses pull up about every ten minutes.
PARKING: Parking around the side of Carolwood.

The Black Dahlia

Various locations

Locations related to the famous cold case.

The number of famous and fascinating crimes that have taken place in Los Angeles is too numerous to list here, but one of the earliest and most gruesome is the case of Elizabeth Short, the so-called Black Dahlia. Popular lore has it that Short was an aspiring actress with a tumultuous past and a taste for the wild life. On the morning of January 15, 1947, Short's naked body was found mutilated and ritually posed in a vacant lot in South Los Angeles. The sensational nature of the crime set off an immediate media frenzy. Local newspapers received mysterious confessions from the purported killer, and more than 150 suspects were questioned. However, no arrests were ever made. To this day, the crime remains unsolved, and many of the details have been obscured into urban legend. Here is a brief list of locations around LA related to the case:

Florentine Gardens (*5951 Hollywood Boulevard, Los Angeles, CA 90028*): Elizabeth Short lived for a brief period in a bungalow behind this then-famous Hollywood hotspot.

Boardners (*1652 North Cherokee Avenue, Los Angeles, CA 90028*): Though often reported that this is where Short took her last drink, that's probably not true. Still, it's a slice of the Black Dahlia's Old Hollywood that's worth a visit.

Millennium Biltmore Hotel (*506 South Grand Avenue, Los Angeles, CA 90071*): One of the last places Short was seen alive. It's said that Short was planning on meeting her sister in the lobby, but that may have been an excuse used to ditch an eager suitor. Her picture is proudly displayed at the hotel alongside other notable guests.

John Sowden House (*5121 Franklin Avenue, Los Angeles, CA 90027*): Many have long suspected that Short's killer may have had specialized medical training due to the precise nature of the dismemberment. LAPD detective Steve Hodel believes his father, surgeon George Hodel, to be the true killer. The Hodels lived in this Lloyd Wright–designed house in the 1940s. Private residence; please do not disturb occupants.

Body Discovery Site (*3825 South Norton Avenue, Los Angeles, CA 90008*): Elizabeth Short's body was found in a vacant lot on this site. At the time, the area was just being developed, but the killer made sure to leave the body prominently where someone would find it. Private residence; please do not disturb occupants.

Cecil Hotel

640 South Main Street, Los Angeles, CA 90014

Accommodations for the infamous.

The Cecil Hotel is the location of so many grim events that it just has to be haunted. The hotel opened in 1924 as budget accommodations for tourists and business travelers. As the area declined, the hotel gained a reputation for depravity and violence. The Skid Row adjacent complex has been the location of at least sixteen suicides or unexplained deaths. Not one but two serial killers are reported to have stayed at the hotel: Night Stalker Richard Ramirez and Austrian Jack Unterweger. In 2013, hotel guest Elisa Lam was found dead floating in the rooftop water tank after acting bizarrely on security camera footage. Today, the Cecil has reopened as an affordable housing complex and was recently deemed a Historical-Cultural Monument by the Los Angeles City Council "for the architecture." The building actually is a nearly intact example of classically influenced Beaux-Arts architecture, and its E-shaped design, allowing for more natural light and air circulation, is considered unique and innovative. The Los Angeles Department of City Planning Historic-Cultural Monument application makes no mention of the hotel's numerous dark connections—a secret identity worth of some of Hotel Cecil's most infamous patrons.

BEST TIME TO GO: Daylight is best to appreciate the architecture, but it's extra creepy at night.

PARKING: Street parking, which is at a premium in downtown, or a pay lot.

Menendez House

722 North Elm Drive, Beverly Hills, CA 90210

Crime scene of family murder.

The late '80s to early 2000s saw an amazing run of true crime and celebrity scandal news stories—O.J. Simpson, Princess Diana, Bill Clinton, Tanya Harding, Mary Kay Letourneau and Erik and Lyle Menendez, two normal kids who killed their parents. On the night of August 20, 1989, the brothers, eighteen and twenty-one, entered the TV room of the family's home with shotguns purchased from a local Big 5 and opened fire on their parents, José and Kitty. In the months after the murders, the brothers spent lavishly, which attracted suspicion from the media and authorities. It wasn't until Erik confessed to his psychiatrist, whose mistress then went to the police, that the crimes caught up with them. The brothers claimed that the violence was self-defense from a lifetime of sexual and physical abuse from their parents, while the prosecution argued that they did it all

The Beverly Hills home of the Menendez family. *Adam Papagan.*

for the money. The jury was deadlocked in their first trial, heavily covered by Court TV. In a second, non-televised trial with a narrower scope of evidence and charges, the brothers were convicted of first-degree murder and sentenced to a lifetime behind bars.

Whether they should be remembered as ruthless, greed-hungry killers or stressed victims pushed to the brink is for you to decide, but this is where it happened. Private residence; please do not disturb occupants.

BEST TIME TO GO: If you want to sync up your visit, the murders occurred sometime after 10:00 p.m. on a Sunday night. Make sure to go around to the back alley for a view of the tennis court where Erik practiced.
PARKING: Plenty of parking right out front.

Halloween
Various locations

Slasher filming locations.

Many consider John Carpenter's *Halloween* an essential contribution to the slasher film genre, and it has been a cult classic since its release in 1978. Although the film takes place on a fall day in the fictional midwestern town of Haddonfield, Illinois, it was actually shot in sunny Southern California (mostly around the quaint neighborhood of South Pasadena). Here's how to find some of the film's more memorable locations.

The Myers House (*1000 Mission Street, South Pasadena*). This is the home featured at the beginning of the film, where a young Michael Myers murders his sister on Halloween night. The home is actually one of South Pasadena's oldest houses and is considered a landmark independent from the film. It was moved to its current location in the late 1980s and has been fully restored. A local art gallery regularly holds film screenings and horror-themed art shows near the location.

Nichol's Hardware (*966 Mission Street, South Pasadena*). This is the store where Michael Myers scores his knife and iconic mask. Fun fact: The original was actually a mask of actor William Shatner painted white.

The iconic hedge from *Halloween* is in South Pasadena. *Adam Papagan.*

LAURIE'S HOUSE (*1115 Oxley Street, South Pasadena*). The home of Jamie Lee Curtis's character has become one of the most recognizable locations in horror. Unlike other film locations, the owners here are proud of their contribution to movie history. Laminated guides with screenshots from the film are left out so visitors can line up the perfect picture. There's even a Styrofoam pumpkin out year-round to pose with. Private residence; please do not disturb occupants.

HADDONFIELD CEMETERY (*Sierra Madre Pioneer Cemetery, 601 East Sierra Madre Boulevard, Sierra Madre*). After visiting the cemetery, it is discovered that the gravestone of Michael's murdered sister, Judith, is missing. This same area can also be seen in Alfred Hitchcock's final film, *Family Plot*, as well as Laura Palmer's funeral in *Twin Peaks*.

THE HEDGE (*Montrose Avenue between Oxley Street and Mission Street, South Pasadena*). Michael Myers conceals himself in these bushes while stalking the film's protagonists. This is maybe one of the most recognizable pieces of shrubbery in all of cinema.

MURPHY RANCH

Sullivan Fire Road, Pacific Palisades, CA 90272

Mysterious ruins from World War II.

There's a whole subcategory of tourism dedicated to exploring abandoned places. The dilapidated Murphy Ranch in the affluent Pacific Palisades neighborhood was built in 1933 by Nazi sympathizers. The property had water storage, barracks and even its own power station. The plan was for the compound to be self-sufficient for long periods of time, as well as serve as a West Coast vacation home for the Führer once he eventually completed his goal of world domination. On December 8, 1941, the day after the attack on Pearl Harbor, the ranch was raided by police, and the property eventually came under the control of the City of Los Angeles. Many of the buildings were torn down in 2016, but you can still explore the graffiti-covered ruins.

BEST TIME TO GO: Mornings. You don't want to be out hiking in the hottest part of the day.
PARKING: Street parking. Read posted signs.

O.J. Simpson
Various locations

The Trial of the Century, visited.

The O.J. Simpson Trial is one of the most famous news events ever to occur in Los Angeles. The trial of disgraced football star O.J. Simpson for the murder of his ex-wife Nicole Brown and her friend Ron Goldman was a daily televised spectacle for much of the mid-1990s and raised questions about the role of celebrity, wealth, race and the media itself in shaping public opinion. Simpson was famously found not guilty despite many people believing that he did it, but the details of the case still spark fascination nearly thirty years later.

Bundy (*879 Bundy Drive, Los Angeles, CA 90049*): This unassuming duplex is the location of one of the most notorious double murders of the twentieth century. Obviously, no one knows exactly what happened, but police believe that Simpson parked in a back alley and stumbled onto the unsuspecting Brown and Goldman, sending him into a rage. The

Nicole Brown Simpson's condo is the location of one of the most publicized news events of the 1990s. *Adam Papagan.*

address and façade of the house have since been changed by the new owners. Private residence; please do not disturb occupants.

Gretna Green Condo (*325 Gretna Green Avenue, Los Angeles, CA 90049*): This is where Nicole lived after separating from O.J. at Rockingham but before moving down to Bundy, where she was murdered. This is where the 911 calls were placed, and you can hear O.J. banging down the door while Nicole pleads with the operator for help. This is also where (if you believe the tabloids) Nicole hooked up with a new boyfriend, knowing that O.J. was in the bushes spying on them. The house on Gretna Green is also the first Los Angeles residence of houseguest Kato Kaelin, who was originally Nicole's friend but sided with O.J. in exchange for nicer, rent-free digs at Rockingham. Private residence; please do not disturb occupants.

Mezzaluna Restaurant (*11750 San Vicente Boulevard, Los Angeles, CA 90049*): This is where Nicole and her family had dinner on the night of the murders and also the workplace of the other victim, Ron Goldman. After dinner, Nicole's mother accidentally left her glasses behind at the restaurant. Waiter Goldman found the glasses and offered to take them over to Nicole's house after work. Officially, Ron and Nicole were just friends, but many suspect that they may have been romantically involved. The Mezzaluna closed in 1997, but it became a total tourist trap during the trial. People would come in to order rigatoni, Nicole's last meal.

Paul Revere Middle School (*1450 Allenford Avenue, Los Angeles, CA 90049*): On the day of the murders, June 12, 1994, O.J. and Nicole's daughter Sydney had a dance recital at Paul Revere Middle School. This came just a few weeks after the couple broke off their latest reconciliation attempt. O.J.'s new girlfriend, Paula Barberi, wanted to come, but O.J., still wanting to get back together with Nicole, told her not to, triggering a breakup that morning. Some accounts say that O.J. was sullen throughout the recital, while others had him in good spirits. Afterward, O.J. approached the Brown family and offered to take everyone out to a big celebratory dinner. Still angry with her former husband, Nicole declined the invitation and said that just the family would go to dinner. Many people speculated that being humiliated by Nicole in public was what set O.J. off on the murderous events of that night.

ROCKINGHAM (*380 Rockingham Avenue, Los Angeles, CA 90049*): This was Simpson's former home, which has long since been torn down and rebuilt. After the murders, O.J. sped home to meet up with the limo driver who was to take him to the airport so that O.J. could catch a flight to Chicago. The limo driver later testified that he saw a dark figure cross the driveway at Rockingham right around 11:00 p.m., possibly Simpson arriving home. This is also where supporters gathered at the culmination of the slow-speed Bronco chase on June 17. Private residence; please do not disturb occupants.

After the murder trial, there was a civil trial where O.J. was found liable for the deaths of Ron and Nicole and ordered to pay millions to the victims' families, triggering the sale of most of his property, including the Rockingham house. I remember very distinctly when the house came down. It was August 8, 1998. I was home from school because it was the summer, watching the local news. They were interviewing people who had come to watch the house be torn down, and one guy was like, "It's a part of history. At home, I have a piece of the Berlin Wall; now I have a piece of O.J.'s house."

HOLLYWOOD FOREVER

6000 Santa Monica Boulevard, Los Angeles, CA 90038

The cenotaph of Johnny Ramone, who is not actually buried here. *Adam Papagan.*

Graveyard know for celebrity burials and movies.

Hollywood Forever gives you the chance to be six feet away from your favorite celebrities. Granted, the celebrities are deceased, but it's exciting nevertheless. Some of Hollywood's biggest names are interred here, including Judy Garland, Douglas Fairbanks, Tyrone Power and Rudolph Valentino. Every year on the anniversary of his death, Valentino's grave is visited by a mysterious "Woman in Black," a tradition dating back to an early Hollywood publicity stunt. The memorials to Johnny Ramone, Burt Reynolds and

Anton Yelchin are easy to spot by the realistic, life-size sculptures on their grave markers. After years of neglect, the cemetery was rebranded around the turn of the twenty-first century. It now regularly holds public events, so you might be able to catch a concert or an outdoor movie projected onto the mausoleum wall. Although celebrities are the big draw, there are many regular folks and aspiring stars here too. One gentleman's epitaph contains the address to his YouTube channel, still hoping for that big break from beyond the grave.

BEST TIME TO GO: Great for a picnic. The staff is really nice about letting people hang out there.
PARKING: Free parking at the cemetery. During events, they charge for parking, but you might be able to find something on Santa Monica Boulevard.

Los Feliz Murder House

2475 Glendower Place, Los Angeles, CA 90027

A real haunted house on the edge of Griffith Park.

The kind of things that only happen in the movies really happen in Los Angeles. *The Fresh Prince of Bel-Air*—really happened to the series creator. *Indiana Jones*—based on a real guy from Echo Park. And the Los Feliz neighborhood is home to an honest-to-goodness haunted house. The Los Feliz Murder Mansion, as locals know it, was the site of a grisly murder-suicide in 1956 in which Dr. Harold Perelson murdered his wife with a ball-peen hammer and attempted to murder his eldest daughter before ingesting poison and killing himself. Urban legend held that the house was abandoned, with all of the family's belongings left untouched inside. Before word got out, it was pretty easy to snoop around and explore the property. There was a crumbling birdbath and sheets over the furniture, just like in a movie. You could see unopened Christmas presents through one of the windows. The specter of Frank Lloyd Wright's Ennis House on the hillside above adds to the foreboding nature. Years later, it came out that the house was being used for storage, and there were tenants who lived in the house after the Perelsons for thirty years, but it's still really creepy. A new owner put a fence around the property a few years ago, but the house is still chilling from the streets. The mansion is likely fated to finally be torn

The Los Feliz Murder House was abandoned decades ago. *Adam Papagan.*

down, but for now, it stands as a literal House on Haunted Hill. Private residence; please do not disturb occupants.

BEST TIME TO GO: Scary during the day, scarier at night.
PARKING: Street parking. Expect dirty looks from the neighbors.

Santa Monica Courthouse

1725 Main Street, Santa Monica, CA 90401

Where celebrities and the justice system meet.

It's a common cliché: "Celebrities, they're just like us!" However, celebrities seem to get into a bit more trouble with the law than the average person. Given its proximity to the more affluent West Los Angeles, the Santa Monica Courthouse has been the setting of a number of high-profile celebrity trials. This is the location of the untelevised O.J. Simpson civil trial in 1996. Roman Polanski also faced rape charges here before famously fleeing the country. Winona Ryder, Lindsay Lohan, Paula Poundstone, Bill Cosby and Christian Brando have also faced the judge here. A number of celebrity divorces were

The Santa Monica Courthouse has been the setting of many celebrity trials. *John Margolis.*

finalized here as well, including Marilyn Monroe's split from Joe DiMaggio. In high school, I got in trouble for smoking and had to appear in front of a juvenile judge in this very building. Maybe celebrities are like us after all.

BEST TIME TO GO: Preferably not while standing trial.
PARKING: There's a lot for people actually going to court or with other government businesses.

PIERCE BROTHERS WESTWOOD CEMETERY

1218 Glendon Avenue, Los Angeles, CA 90024

Star-studded burial ground.

The compact Pierce Brothers cemetery in Westwood is probably the highest concentration of celebrity graves anywhere. The cemetery has been active since the 1880s but did not become famous until Marilyn Monroe was interred there. Joe DiMaggio was in charge of her funeral arrangements and picked Westwood because of its low profile. However, with Marilyn's presence, the graveyard quickly became fashionable. Today, there's no shortage of celebrities, and it's easy to spot the graves of Jack Lemon,

Westwood Cemetery features an impressive number of celebrity graves for its size. *Carol Highsmith.*

Farrah Fawcett, Truman Capote, Merv Griffin, Billy Wilder, Natalie Wood and many others. An informal tradition has arisen of leaving a joke as an epitaph. My favorite is from comedian Rodney Dangerfield—"There goes the neighborhood."

BEST TIME TO GO: Although the hours listed say twenty-four hours, it usually closes up around sundown.
PARKING: Just drive in and you can kind of park wherever.

Nightmare on Elm Street

1428 Genesee Avenue, Los Angeles, CA 900346

Real filming location for classic horror movie.

The town of Springwood, Ohio, the setting of the original *Nightmare on Elm Street* film, is actually in the heart of Hollywood. The colonial house featured in the iconic first Freddy Krueger movie is just off Sunset Boulevard. The name of the street was changed because *Nightmare on Genesee Avenue* just doesn't have the same ring to it. Interestingly, some of the houses featured in *Halloween* are just around the corner on Orange Grove Avenue. Another bizarre coincidence—Elm Drive in Beverly Hills, a few miles away, is the location of the real-life Menendez murders. Sleep tight. Private residence; please do not disturb occupants.

BEST TIME TO GO: Easier to see during the day but scarier at night.
PARKING: Street parking.

Manson

Various locations

LA's most infamous death cult.

The story of Charles Manson and his "family" of crazed hippies is one of the most well-known true crime events ever to take place in Los Angeles. The official narrative paints Manson as a criminal mastermind who duped his unsuspecting young followers into killing actress Sharon Tate and eight others in a multi-day killing spree in order to incite a race war. There's likely more to the story, but the "technically, he never killed anyone" argument is not for this book. There are many books and documentaries that delve into all the alternative theories, but for now here's a list of locations important to the case.

Hinnman House (*964 Old Topanga Canyon Road, Topanga, CA 90290*): A week and a half before the Tate/LaBianca murders, music teacher Gary Hinnman, an associate of the Family, was found murdered in his home. Authorities later suspected that the crimes may be linked. Private residence; please do not disturb occupants.

Tate House (*10066 Cielo Drive, Beverly Hills, CA 90210*): This is the address of the home where the pregnant Sharon Tate, along with her friends Jay Sebring, Abigail Folger, Voytek Frykowski and passerby Steven Parent, were murdered. The original house was torn down in the '90s, but "fans" still make pilgrimages to this site. Private residence; please do not disturb occupants.

LaBianca House (*3311 Waverly Drive, Los Angeles, CA 90027*): The next night, the Family, this time accompanied by Manson himself, broke into the home of grocery store owner Leno LaBianca and his wife, Rosemary. Manson reportedly tied up the couple and left, leaving his followers to commit the murders and hitchhike home. Private residence; please do not disturb occupants.

Spahn Ranch (*23000 Santa Susana Pass Road, Chatsworth, CA 91311*): Manson and his followers lived in the decaying ruins of the old Spahn Movie Ranch at the time of the murders and immediately after. This is where the famous *Life* magazine photos were taken and where part of the Manson documentary was filmed. Amazingly, this land is now Santa Susana State Park and open to the public.

The "27 Club"

Various locations

A rock-and-roll club you don't want to enter.

The "27 Club" is the name given to the informal list of great artists who tragically passed away at the age of twenty-seven. Members with this dubious distinction include Amy Winehouse, Janis Joplin, Jim Morrison, Jimi Hendrix, Kurt Cobain and original Rolling Stone Brian Jones. Despite not living very long, many 27 Clubbers spent key moments in their very short lives in Los Angeles. Following is a list of places where you can retrace the steps of the 27 Club.

Jonathan Brandis Apartment (*650 South Detroit Street, Los Angeles, CA 90036 #20*): Teen actor Jonathan Brandis was best known for his role as teen prodigy Lucas Wolenczak on the NBC series *SeaQuest DSV*. At the height of his fame, the actor received four thousand fan letters per week, but those days were long behind him when he committed suicide by hanging himself on a beam in the hallway of his apartment building while his friends partied inside. They thought that he had turned in for the night. Jonathan did not leave a suicide note, but after his death, his friends reported that he had been depressed about his extended career lull. His father revealed in 2021 that Jonathan was probably suffering from bipolar disorder. Private residence; please do not disturb occupants.

Kurt Cobain House (*6681 Alta Loma Terrace. Los Angeles, CA 90068*): Nirvana frontman Kurt Cobain had two main residences in Los Angeles. The first was a small apartment in the Melrose area. It's depicted in

A mural depicting 27 Club member Jim Morrison. *Adam Papagan.*

the documentary *Montage of Heck* as little more than a drug den with mattresses on the floor and trash strewn about. The second was a peculiar house not far from Hollywood Boulevard. The Alta Loma house is in the High Tower neighborhood, which is accessible only by a private elevator or a steep set of public stairs. Kurt could have possibly picked the secluded location in an effort to hide away from his sudden and unwanted fame. The house has been unoccupied for years, and fans have subtly begun leaving tributes around the exterior of the home. Private residence; please do not disturb occupants.

JANIS JOPLIN DEATH SITE (*Highland Gardens Hotel, 7047 Franklin Avenue, Los Angeles, CA 90028*): Blues singer Janis Joplin is another member of the 27 Club. While recording what would end up being her final album, *Pearl*, at Sunset Sound, Joplin rented a large room at this hotel. One night, she looked out her window, saw a heroin dealer at the park across the street and decided she needed a fix. Joplin had apparently only been a heroin user for a few weeks, and the dealer hooked her up with a particularly strong batch she was not prepared for. She overdosed later that night. The hotel has been converted into transitional housing for people experiencing homelessness, but the room has been sealed off and preserved.

JIM MORRISON'S PANTS (*Hard Rock Café, 6801 Hollywood Boulevard, Suite 105, Los Angeles, CA 90028*): There's no shortage of Doors landmarks around town, but one of the most intriguing is Jim Morrison's leather pants. Morrison wore these pants on and off stage. You'll definitely recognize them from classic photographs and footage of the Doors performing. Jim is believed to have worn the pants every day for two years. Considering how long he lived, that's a good chunk of his life spent wearing these pants.

ANTON YELCHIN GRAVE (*Hollywood Forever, 6000 Santa Monica Boulevard, Los Angeles, CA 90038*): Anton Yelchin was a promising young actor. He began his career as a child and, by his mid-twenties, had appeared in more than forty films. One day, on his way out of the house for a rehearsal, he parked his Jeep Grand Cherokee at the top of his steep driveway and got out to check his mail. In a freak accident, the car rolled backward, pinning him against a gate and causing him to asphyxiate. Yelchin is interred at Hollywood Forever Cemetery in a monument adorned with a nearly life-size bronze statue. His epitaph reads, "Anton Yelchin: 1989–Forever."

Chapter 10

ODD LA

I once led a reality television–themed sightseeing tour for a group of enthusiastic *Real Housewives* fans, as well as one grumpy older gentleman who I think booked the tour by mistake. While the other guests gushed over the latest gossip about Lisa Rinna and Erika Jayne, the man just sat there totally befuddled. As he exited the tour vehicle, I heard him mutter, "California—the land of fruits and nuts!"

I think he meant it to be derogatory, but around here we take stuff like that as a compliment. LA is an all-around weird place. Our eclectic population, unique industries and disorienting geography make everything just a little bit strange to the point where you stop to notice it. Los Angeles is teeming with unusual places. Sites that would be major oddities in other towns can sometimes even fly under the radar. Here are some of my favorite attractions that are odd even for LA.

The Bunny Museum

2605 Lake Avenue, Altadena, CA 91001

The definitive source on all things bunny.

The Bunny Museum was one of the weirdest museums in LA or anywhere. The museum was founded by husband and wife Steve Lubanski and Candace

Bunny offerings left at the entrance to the Bunny Museum. *Adam Papagan.*

Frazee, who started collecting rabbit-themed items after their first Valentine's Day together. Initially located inside the couple's own home, the museum was expanded to its own facility containing more than forty thousand stuffed animals, figurines, cookie jars, posters, toys and other bunny-related items. Although the museum was ostensibly dedicated to bunnies, tributes to Candace and Steve are everywhere. The couple's wedding photos were scattered throughout the collection, along with a re-creation of their home kitchen and several books Candace has written about the Swedenborgian religion. Annual membership included admission for two into their "night parties." In early 2025, the area where the museum is located was devastated by the Eaton Fire. The Bunny Museum and many other beloved local businesses were lost in the blaze. Undeterred, Candace, who now refers to the entire disaster as the "Bunny Museum Fire," has vowed to rebuild with more bunny items than ever.

BEST TIME TO GO: Great date spot. They go all out for Easter and Valentine's Day.
PARKING: Street parking.

La Brea Tar Pits

5801 Wilshire Boulevard, Los Angeles, CA 90036

A natural phenomenon on Wilshire.

This is a location truly unique to Los Angeles, but it has nothing to do with show business, architecture or true crime. A tar pit, or asphalt lake, is a geologic phenomenon occurring only in a few places in the world (the others being Trinidad, Venezuela, Azerbaijan, Oklahoma and two additional ones in Bakersfield and Carpinteria, California). I'm still a bit confused about the science, but basically, crude oil from the ground seeps up to the surface and partially evaporates, leaving a sticky tar that traps animals. Predators will prey on the helpless animals, becoming trapped themselves. As the tar envelopes the animals, it preserves the bones, creating a fossil. Since the tar pits lie in the middle of Wilshire Boulevard, one of the busiest streets in the city, thousands of artifacts have been found as the area has been built up. Many of these fossils of mammoths, dire wolves and sabretooth cats can be found in the adjacent George C. Page Museum, but viewing the actual tar pits is free. Only once has a guest been underwhelmed by a visit to the tar pits. He was from Trinidad, one of the only other places on the planet where a prehistoric tar pit is a common sight.

BEST TIME TO GO: The grounds close at night, but the tar pits are easily viewable from Wilshire Boulevard.
PARKING: You can usually find a meter or even free parking on 6th Street.

The Pink Wall

8221 Melrose Avenue, Los Angeles, CA 90046

A clothing store famous for the building's hue.

Designer Paul Smith wanted his flagship Melrose boutique to be a landmark as recognizable as the Eiffel Tower, so he painted the entire building bright pink. The exact hue is specially formulated and copyrighted, so you'll only find it here. Although the wall itself predates Instagram, it wasn't long before influencers realized how good they looked photographed in front of it. Now tens of thousands of people a year from across the world visit the wall and take selfies. It costs the store about $60,000 a year to maintain the wall, but for the Eiffel Tower of walls, it's well worth it.

BEST TIME TO GO: Does not photograph as well at night.
PARKING: There's a lot, but there's an attendant, so if you're just there to take photos, try to grab a meter.

Los Angeles Live Steamers Railroad Museum and Walt's Barn

5202 Zoo Drive, Los Angeles, CA 90027

Model trains and a free Disney experience.

"Live Steamers" are model railroad enthusiasts who build and run scaled-down steam-powered locomotives. Their Griffith Park headquarters contains a nice collection of models and layouts, but the real draw is Walt Disney's personal backyard barn, where he himself ran model railroads. The barn was originally Walt's workshop at his Holmby Hills home on Carolwood Drive. Walt would tinker in the barn, dreaming of one day having an even larger model railroad to play with. Before long, the seeds were planted for what would become Disneyland. The barn was moved to the Live Steamers property by the family in the late '90s and is used to display numerous Disneyland-related artifacts. This is believed to be the only free Disney attraction in the world, which is notable in and of itself and is definitely the only Disney attraction with free parking.

BEST TIME TO GO: It's only open one Sunday a month, but if your schedule allows, it's well worth a visit.
PARKING: Free parking along Zoo Drive.

Scientology

Various locations

People see the Scientology buildings around Hollywood and always have questions. In the interest of avoiding legal action from the church, I'll just say that Hollywood wouldn't be the same without them.

BEST TIME TO GO: N/A.
PARKING: N/A.

Urban Oil Fields

Various locations

Active oil extraction in the middle of the city.

The Pico Drill Site once contained an informative exhibit about oil extraction in its lobby that has since been closed. *Adam Papagan.*

Did you know Southern California is the largest oil field west of Texas? Active oil wells are scattered throughout the Los Angeles area. In some areas, like La Cienega, they're right out in the open between otherwise normal residential neighborhoods. In other areas, they go to great lengths to conceal them. The Beverly Center Mall is situated on top of a number of active wells that the building's fortress-like construction was designed to conceal. There's also one on the grounds of Beverly Hills High School, conspicuously concealed under a giant floral printed sock. In the Pico Robertson neighborhood, a heavily Jewish area, there's one built to look like a synagogue. A little farther down the street on Pico and Fairfax, there's a large, tan, windowless building meant to conceal another large well. There's no roof on the building, and instead, the four walls are a massive façade built to blend into the surrounding neighborhood. It's not the kind of thing they really want you to know about, but now you do.

BEST TIME TO GO: Not something you go to per se, but rather something that's all around.

PARKING: N/A.

Magic Castle

7001 Franklin Avenue, Los Angeles, CA 90028

A private club unlike any in the world.

There's a lot of talk about metaphorical Hollywood magic, but the Magic Castle is the literal home of the magical arts in Hollywood. The Magic Castle is a private club for magicians and magic enthusiasts. To gain entrance, you must be a member or invited by a member, although if you stay at the adjoining hotel someone can usually hook you up. There is a strict formal dress code and photography is not allowed, but inside you will find secret passageways, a full-service restaurant and performance spaces for everything from card tricks to elaborate stage magic. The structure itself features many obscure architectural details. Club founder Milt Larsen had a routine of ransacking Victorian buildings slated for demolition and installing the best bits at the castle. It's all a little corny, but it's a fun night out if you can get in. After visiting the club's many bars, you may find that most of your money has disappeared. Tada!

BEST TIME TO GO: Shows seven nights a week, but it's more happening on the weekends.
PARKING: Valet. The castle is up a steep hill, so if you go for street parking, you have to walk up the driveway in your formal wear, which is a tad embarrassing.

Berlin Wall Segment

5900 Wilshire Boulevard, Los Angeles, CA 90036

Cold War relic relocated to the City of Angels.

The largest segment of the Berlin Wall outside of Germany is across the street from the La Brea Tar Pits. The ten segments were brought to Los Angeles in 2009 by the Wende Museum to commemorate the twentieth anniversary of the wall coming down. The museum then commissioned several well-known and emerging artists to paint the wall, including Thierry Noir, a French-born artist who was one of the first artists to paint on the Berlin Wall in 1984. Several of the segments have been unchanged, showcasing the original Cold War–era graffiti. The Wende has a full museum across town in Culver City, but the wall is the main thing you'll want to check out.

BEST TIME TO GO: Never crowded. In fact, most people don't even know it's there.
PARKING: Occasionally, there are meters on Wilshire, and at certain times of day, it's easy to double park if you just want to take a quick picture.

The Old Zoo

4801 Griffith Park Drive, Los Angeles, CA 90027

Experience what it's like to be a Depression-era zoo animal.

Griffith Park has a lot to do—there's a carousel, museums, a zoo and the ruins of an old zoo that they let you climb around on. The original Griffith Park Zoo dates back to 1912 and held just fifteen animals. In the 1930s, a WPA project expanded the zoo, and several caged-in, cave-like structures were built. However, conditions at the zoo began to deteriorate, and funds were raised for a new Los Angeles Zoo a few miles away. The animals were moved to the new zoo in 1966, and the old zoo was left essentially intact as a recreation area. There are a few picnic tables and hiking trails leading around the habitats. Some of the bars have been removed, and it's easy to slip inside the unlocked cages, even if the small enclosures do make you feel bad for the animals who used to live in them.

BEST TIME TO GO: LA gets hot in the summer, so try to do any hiking in the morning.
PARKING: Parking lot.

The Witch's House

516 Walden Drive, Beverly Hills, CA 90210

Atypical Beverly Hills landmark.

Italian villas, Spanish missions, Tudor castles—the architecture in Beverly Hills is like taking a trip around the world. One of the most unique of these personalized properties is the Witch's House. Officially called the Spadena House, the whimsical home looks like something out of a fairy tale, which isn't too far off. The house was designed by Hollywood art director Harry Oliver, originally as an office and dressing room at a Culver City movie studio. It was moved to this location in 1926 and expanded into an actual house. Many see it as a precursor to the theme parks that came later, whereby fanciful environments are developed into actual places. The Witch's House has been declared a historic landmark, meaning this unique property will be a part of the character of Beverly Hills for years to come. Private residence; please do not disturb occupants.

The Witch's House is a popular Beverly Hills attraction, particularly around Halloween. *Carol Highsmith.*

BEST TIME TO GO: You'd think it would be cooler at night, but they don't really light it up, so it's better to visit during the day.
PARKING: Street parking.

AFTERWORD

When real estate investors first tried to sell potential new residents on Southern California, it was pitched as place with abundant, inexpensive land, limitless financial opportunity and a lush Mediterranean climate beneficial for numerous chronic health conditions. Nearly a century and a half later, we've ended up with an endless stretch of unaffordable concrete, impassible traffic on our streets and highways and chronically poor air quality. One of the most beautiful, biodiverse landscapes in the world has been rendered a harsh urban wasteland. It's a twist so dramatic it could have come out of a Hollywood movie.

So, how can one city with so many identities continue to fascinate the world year after year? The answer is the people. Every story in this book, every interesting thing about Los Angeles, is the result of the people who call this place home. You can find every kind of person here—innovators and plagiarists, idols and addicts, heroes and villains. It's really the unique people here who make it a unique place. While no one knows what changes may come, thanks to its people, I'm confident that Los Angeles will always be Los Angeles.

BIBLIOGRAPHY

Notable Streets and Neighborhoods

About Hollywood. "Hollywood History and Information." November 16, 2010. https://web.archive.org/web/20110418010207/http://www.abouthollywood.com/hollywood-neighborhoods/hollywood-california-history-and-information.

Baum, Gary. "Why Century City Ranks Among the Worst Real Estate Deals in Hollywood History." *Hollywood Reporter*, September 26, 2013. http://www.hollywoodreporter.com/news/why-century-city-ranks-worst-635438.

Blake, Lindsay. "Scene It Before: The Thriller House." *Los Angeles Magazine* (October 30, 2014). https://lamag.com/film/scene-thriller-house.

Bogdanovich, Peter, dir. *Tom Petty and the Heartbreakers: Runnin' Down a Dream*. 2007.

City of Los Angeles. "Angelino Heights Preservation Plan." June 10, 2004. LACity.org.

Cross, Justin. "7 Amazing Street Performers You'll See on the Venice Beach Boardwalk." TimeOut, June 12, 2015. https://www.timeout.com/los-angeles/blog/7-amazing-street-performers-youll-see-on-the-venice-beach-boardwalk.

Deutch, Joann. "What's That at Laurel Canyon and Lookout Mountain?" *Canyon News*, May 4, 2008. https://web.archive.org/web/20111117221209/http://www.canyon-news.com/artman2/publish/DegreesCoolerfeb/What_s_that_at_Laurel_Canyon_and_Lookout_Mountain.php.

Do, Anh. "Mutual Aid Clubs Are Still Going Strong in L.A. Chinatown. But Their Future Is Uncertain." *Los Angeles Times*, April 2, 2023. https://www.latimes.com/california/story/2023-04-02/chinese-benevolent-associations-los-angeles.

Echo Park Historical Society. "Historic Echo Park." https://www.historicechopark.org/blog-1-2/echo-park-lake.

French, Philip. "How 100 Years of Hollywood Have Charted the History of America." *Guardian*, February 28, 2010. https://www.theguardian.com/film/2010/feb/28/philip-french-best-hollywood-films.

Gordon, Larry. "Echo Park Lake Reopens After Two-Year Makeover." *Los Angeles Times*, June 15, 2013. https://www.latimes.com/local/la-xpm-2013-jun-15-la-me-0616-echopark-lake-20130616-story.html.

Green, Terence. "2nd Little Tokyo Mall to Get Under Way." *Los Angeles Times*, November 12, 1978. https://www.newspapers.com/clip/44154830/ewdc-weller-court.

Henstell, Bruce. *Sunshine and Wealth: Los Angeles in the Twenties and Thirties*. Chronicle Books, 1984.

Howser, Huell, prod. *Our Neighborhoods*. "Angelino Heights." KCET, October 3, 2002.

Huffman, John Pearley. "The Sunset Strip Has Been a Moving Nightly Party for Nearly a Century." *Road & Track*, April 12, 2022. https://www.roadandtrack.com/car-culture/a39529791/the-sunset-strip-has-been-a-moving-nightly-party-for-nearly-a-century.

Jennings, Angel, and Paloma Esquivel. "'Straight Outta' a Different Compton: City Says Much Has Changed in 25 Years." *Los Angeles Times*, August 14, 2015. https://web.archive.org/web/20200514224713/https://www.latimes.com/local/california/la-me-0815-compton-image-20150815-story.html.

Kropp, Phoebe. "Citizens of the Past?: Olvera Street and the Construction of Race and Memory in 1930s Los Angeles." *Radical History Review* 81 (2001): 34–60. doi:10.1215/01636545-2001-81-34. S2CID 143936420. https://www.semanticscholar.org/paper/Citizens-of-the-Past%3A-Olvera-Street-and-the-of-Race-Kropp/0174b96cf775ea78370de9b00393473c4ae55d51.

Larson, Louise. "Colorful Pioneer of Malibu Inured." *Evening Outlook*, December 15, 1970.

Lombard, Patricia. "Neighbors Celebrate Beverly Fairfax Historic District." *Larchmont Buzz*, August 8, 2013. https://larchmontbuzz.com/larchmont-village-hancock-park-real-estate/neighbors-celebrate-beverly-fairfax-historic-district.

Los Angeles Almanac. "Population of Communities of the City of Los Angeles." January 11, 2010. https://web.archive.org/web/20100111043420/http://www.laalmanac.com/population/po24la.htm.

Malibu House. "Malibu, California: A Star in Its Own Right on the Screen." June 7, 2024. https://malibu.house/blog/2024/06/07/malibu-california-a-star-in-its-own-right-on-the-screen.

McClain, James. "YouTubers Ethan & Hilda Klein Buy $9 Million Bel Air Mansion." *DIRT*, October 28, 2019. https://www.dirt.com/entertainers/influencers/ethan-klein-house-bel-air-1203300328.

Melton, Mary. "The Stars of Star Maps." *Los Angeles Times*, August 25, 1996. https://articles.latimes.com/1996-08-25/magazine/tm-37374_1_movie-star-map.

Morrison, Patt. "Griffith Park Is Named for a Guy Who Shot His Wife—and Other True Stories of L.A. Parks." *Los Angeles Times*, May 3, 2022. https://www.latimes.com/california/story/2022-05-03/la-parks-names-griffith-runyon-debs.

Mountains Recreation and Conservation Authority. "Universal City Overlook." https://mrca.ca.gov/parks/park-listing/universal-city-overlook.

Mulholland, Catherine. *William Mulholland and the Rise of Los Angeles*. University of California Press, 2002.

Palmer, Karen. "One of America's Last Japantowns Is in Trouble." *SFGate*, June 7, 2024. https://www.sfgate.com/la/article/little-tokyo-los-angeles-endangered-restaurants-19463905.php.

Parra, Alvaro. "Olvera Street: The Fabrication of L.A.'s Mexican Heritage." KCET, September 13, 2013. https://www.pbssocal.org/history-society/olvera-street-the-fabrication-of-l-a-s-mexican-heritage.

Pool, Bob. "Turning the Corner at Hollywood and Vine." *Los Angeles Times*, May 4, 2008. http://www.latimes.com/news/local/la-me-thenandnow4-2008may04,0,2431816.story.

Quon, Cameron. "Chinatown: The Tale of Three Plazas." Annenberg TV News, November 4, 2015. https://web.archive.org/web/20160127155142/http://www.atvn.org/news/2015/11/chinatown.

Rode, Erin. "There's a Secret Mystery Forest in the Middle of This Big City Park." *SFGate*, January 26, 2024. https://www.sfgate.com/la/article/california-griffith-park-forest-hike-18621449.php.

Roth, Matthew W. "Mulholland Highway and the Engineering Culture of Los Angeles in the 1920s." *Technology and Culture* 40 (July 1999): 545–75.

Shyong, Frank. "Bruce Lee Statue Unveiled in L.A.'s Chinatown." *Los Angeles Times*, June 16, 2013. http://www.latimes.com/local/lanow/la-me-ln-bruce-lee-statue-unveiled-in-las-chinatown-20130616,0,4835552.story.

Stanton, Jeffrey. "Debunking Venice's Historic Myths." Venice History Site, April 22, 2019. https://www.westland.net/venicehistory/articles/myths.htm.

Sudhalter, Kim. "Have You Ever Wondered…Why Sunset + Vine Has a Streamline Moderne Facade?" Hollywood Partnership, December 16, 2014. https://hollywoodpartnership.com/post/ever-wondered-sunset-vine-streamline-moderne-facade.

Tapley, Kristopher. "'Die Hard' Celebrates 30th Anniversary with Outdoor 'Nakatomi Tower' Screening." *Variety*, July 29, 2018. https://variety.com/2018/film/news/die-hard-30th-anniversary-nakatomi-tower-screening-1202889427.

Trust for Public Land. "The 150 Largest City Parks." December 10, 2010.

U.S. Census Bureau. "U.S. Census Bureau QuickFacts: Compton City, California." 2023. https://www.census.gov/quickfacts/fact/table/comptoncitycalifornia/PST045222.

Weller, Sheila. *Girls Like Us: Carole King, Joni Mitchell, Carly Simon—And the Journey of a Generation.* Atria Books, 2008.

Yu, Eui-Young, Pater Choe, Sang Il Han and Kimberly Yu. "Emerging Diversity, Los Angeles' Koreatown 1990–2000." *Amerasia Journal* 30, no. 1 (2004): 25–52. doi:10.17953/amer.30.1.m470332320241t24. S2CID 147663578. https://api.semanticscholar.org/CorpusID:147663578.

Buildings and Infrastructure

Begley, Sarah. "The Most Popular Places to Check In on Facebook in 2015." *Time* (December 10, 2015). http://time.com/4144194/these-were-the-most-popular-places-to-check-in-on-facebook-in-2015.

Beverly Hills Historical Society. "A Brief History of Beverly Hills." *https*://www.beverlyhillshistoricalsociety.org/history.

Bottles, Scott. *Los Angeles and the Automobile: The Making of the Modern City*. University of California Press, 1987.

Branudy, Leo. *The Hollywood Sign*. Yale University Press 2011.

California State Parks. "Watts Towers." Office of Historic Preservation, California State Parks. http://ohp.parks.ca.gov/ListedResources/Detail/993.

Carlson, Jen. "A Brief History of L.A.'s Beautiful Union Station." LAist, April 12, 2016. https://web.archive.org/web/20190812173847/https://laist.com/2016/04/12/union_station_history.php.

Chiland, Elijah. "Preservationists Raise Concerns About Crossroads of the World Redevelopment: 'We're Headed to Manhattanization of Hollywood.'" Curbed LA, September 7, 2017. https://la.curbed.com/2017/9/7/16269146/los-angeles-crossroads-of-the-world-hollywood-project-historic-preservation.

City of Los Angeles. http://webarchive.loc.gov/all/20101113064227/http://www.lacity.org/YourGovernment/CityCouncil/index.htm.

Daunt, Tina. "Elton John's Oscar Party Raises Nearly $4 Million." *Los Angeles Times*, February 24, 2009. http://articles.latimes.com/2009/feb/24/entertainment/et-cause24.

DiMassa, Cara Mia. "Angels Flight Rides Again." *Los Angeles Times*, March 15, 2010. https://www.latimes.com/news/local/la-me-angels-flight16-2010mar16,0,814117.story.

Gettell, Oliver. "Cinerama Dome Puts 'How the West Was Won' in Proper Perspective." *Los Angeles Times*, April 12, 2012. http://articles.latimes.com/2012/apr/12/entertainment/la-et-0412-cinerama-20120412.

Gross, Michael. *Unreal Estate: Money, Ambition, and the Lust for Land in Los Angeles*. Random House Digital Inc., 2011.

Hollywood Reporter. "John Ritter Photo Added to Mural." June 5, 2008. https://web.archive.org/web/20080608082627/http://www.hollywoodreporter.com/hr/content_display/features/people/e3iaeef9cc73853f3d00ededed1d47c9976.

LA Conservancy. "Four-Level Interchange." https://www.laconservancy.org/locations/four-level-interchange.

Los Angeles Times. "Hollywood High Named to Register of Historic Places." January 23, 2012. http://latimesblogs.latimes.com/lanow/2012/01/hollywood-high-named-to-historic-places-register.html.

———. "LAPD Unit to Move to Historic Building." February 13, 1996. http://articles.latimes.com/1996-02-13/local/me-35412_1_bradbury-building.

Lyons, Carolyn. "Watts Towers: LA's Weird Masterpiece." *Guardian*, August 25, 2011. https://www.theguardian.com/travel/2011/aug/25/watts-tower-los-angeles-sculpture.

Maddaus, Gene. "Why Did the ArcLight Fade Away? Inside the Sad Final Chapter of the Pacific Theatres Chain." *Variety*, June 15, 2021. https://variety.com/2021/film/news/arclight-cinerama-dome-pacific-theatres-chris-forman-1234996192.

Magruder, Melonie. "Pacific Park Celebrates 15th Birthday." Surf Santa Monica, June 2, 2011. https://www.surfsantamonica.com/ssm_site/the_lookout/news/News-2011/June-2011/06_02_2011_Pacific_Park_Celebrates_15th_Birthday.htm.

Masters, Nathan. "L.A.'s Famous Four-Level Freeway Interchange, 'The Stack,' Turns 58." KCET, September 22, 2011. https://www.pbssocal.org/shows/lost-la/l-a-s-famous-four-level-freeway-interchange-the-stack-turns-58.

———. "The Lost Canals of Venice of America." KCET, April 5, 2013. http://www.kcet.org/updaily/socal_focus/history/la-as-subject/the-lost-canals-of-venice-of-america.html.

Muchnic, Suzanne. "An Artful Addition to Bradbury's Interior." *Los Angeles Times*, June 24, 2007. http://articles.latimes.com/2007/jun/24/entertainment/ca-Chinese24.

Oswald, Anjelica. "Stan Lee, Marvel Legend, Dead at 95." *Business Insider*, November 12, 2018. https://www.businessinsider.com/stan-lee-dead-marvel-2018-10.

Ryon, Ruth. "Brown Derby to Crown New Shopping Plaza." *Los Angeles Times*, May 19, 1985. http://articles.latimes.com/1985-05-19/realestate/re-9531_1_brown-derby.

Schaefer, Samantha. "Angels Flight Car Comes Off Track, Stranding Australian Tourist." *Los Angeles Times*, September 5, 2013. https://www.latimes.com/local/la-me-angels-flight-20130906,0,3692857.story.

Scheuer, Philip K. "A Town Called Hollywood." *Los Angeles Times*, May 10, 1936. https://search.proquest.com/docview/164618483.

Schneider, Jerry L. *Western Filming Locations California: Book 3*. Barnes and Noble Press, 2015.

Smith, Leon. *Hollywood Goes on Location*. Pomegranate Press, 1988.

Solomons, Gabriel. *World Film Locations: Los Angeles*. Intellect Books, 2011.

Sudhalter, Kim. "Have You Ever Wondered…What the Crossroads of the World Is All About?" Only in Hollywood, December 1, 2014. http://onlyinhollywood.org/ever-wondered-crossroads-world.

U.S. News & World Report. "America's Best Hospitals: The 2022–2023 Honor Roll and Overview." July 26, 2022. https://health.usnews.com/health-care/best-hospitals/articles/best-hospitals-honor-roll-and-overview.

Vankin, Deborah. "Abstract Frank Stella Sculpture 'Adjoeman' Joins Cedars-Sinai Artworks." *Los Angeles Times*, July 7, 2014. https://www.latimes.com/entertainment/arts/la-et-cm-cedars-art-stella-20140707-story.html.

Vincent, Roger. "Red Building at Pacific Design Center Getting Tenants at Last." *Los Angeles Times*, March 26, 2015. http://www.latimes.com/business/la-fi-0326-property-report-red-building-20150326-story.html.

Wick, Julia. "City Hall Was L.A.'s Tallest Building for 4 Decades—By Law." *LAist*, April 26, 2016. https://laist.com/news/entertainment/city-hall-tall.

Yogananda, Paramahansa. "49: The Years 1940–1951." *Autobiography of a Yogi*. MIF Books & the Philosophical Library Inc., 1946.

Prominent Properties

Amelar, Sarah. "Two Eames Grandchildren on Charles and Ray's Living Room." *New York Times*, October 5, 2011. https://www.nytimes.com/2011/10/06/garden/the-eames-house-living-room.html.

Beverly Hills Courier. "Six Beverly Hills Properties Named Local Historic Landmarks." January 30, 2013. http://bhcourier.com/beverly-hills-properties-named-local-historic-landmarks/2013/01/30.

Bosley, Edward R. *Gamble House: Greene and Greene*. Phaidon, 1992.

Brown, John, and James Boyd. *History of San Bernardino and Riverside Counties*. Western Historical Association, 1922.

Cowan, Jared. "The Gamble House Goes Back to the Future." *LA Weekly*, July 26, 2015.

Daily Telegraph. "The Top Houses from the Movies." May 2, 2012. https://web.archive.org/web/20120502235333/http://www.telegraph.co.uk/property/propertypicturegalleries/9239346/The-top-houses-from-the-movies.html.

Hart, John. "Los Angeles Home Spotlight: The O'Neill House Isn't Like Other Beverly Hills Homes." April 18, 2023. johnhartrealestate.com.

Hawthorne, Christopher. "New Getty Initiative Aims to Boost Preservation of Modern Architecture." *Los Angeles Times*, March 21, 2012. http://latimesblogs.latimes.com/culturemonster/2012/03/getty-modern-architecture-preservation-eames-house.html.

Hobart, Christy. "At Greystone, There Will Be 'Blood'—and Bowling." *Los Angeles Times*, December 27, 2007. http://www.latimes.com/features/home/la-hm-blood27dec27,1,6977925.story?ctrack=2&cset=true.

Martin, Hugo. "How I Made It: Vahid Sapir." *Los Angeles Times*, January 17, 2010. https://www.latimes.com/archives/la-xpm-2010-jan-17-la-fi-himi17-2010jan17-story.html.

Mitchell, Sean. "The Best Houses of All Time in L.A." *Los Angeles Times*, December 27, 2008. http://www.latimes.com/features/home/la-hm-besthouse27-pg,0,746372.photogallery.

Muchnic, Suzanne. "The Huntington's Glorious Restoration." *Los Angeles Times*, September 28, 1986. https://articles.latimes.com/1986-09-28/entertainment/ca-9422_1_main-gallery.

———. "Weisman Seeking Another Home for His Art Cache." *Los Angeles Times*, November 14, 1986. http://articles.latimes.com/1986-11-14/entertainment/ca-29422_1_beverly-hills.

Nakano, Craig. "Famed Ennis House Is Sold." *Los Angeles Times*, July 17, 2011. http://www.latimes.com/news/local/la-me-ennis-house-20110717,0,6875474.story.

Robbin, Riley, prod. *Selling Spelling Manor*. Home and Garden Television, December 15, 2011.

Roderick, Kavin. "Case Study Houses Finally Added to National Register." *LA Observed*, August 19, 2013. http://www.laobserved.com/archive/2013/08/case_study_houses_finally.php.

Singleton, Edward. "These Are the 20 Best Parks Los Angeles Has to Offer." *Los Angeles Magazine* (March 9, 2017). https://www.lamag.com/culturefiles/best-parks-los-angeles.

Sozanski, Edward J. "Frederick Weisman Just Can't Get Art Off His Mind." *Chicago Tribune*, June 24, 1987. http://articles.chicagotribune.com/1987-06-24/features/8702160838_1_henry-t-hopkins-corporate-collection-frederick-r-weisman-collection.

Thornburg, Barbara. "Koenig's Case Study House No. 22 as Home." *Los Angeles Times*, June 27, 2009. http://www.latimes.com/features/home/la-hm-stahl27-2009jun27,0,504751.story.

Timberg, Scott. "Landmark Houses: John Lautner's Chemosphere." *Los Angeles Times*, July 23, 2011. http://www.latimes.com/features/home/la-hm-landmark-houses-john-lautner-chemosphere,0,2280421.htmlstory.

Wall Street Journal. "'Selling Spelling Manor': A Peek Inside the Property." December 15, 2011. https://www.wsj.com/articles/BL-SEB-68273.

Museums

ABC7. "L.A. Recognizes Griffith Park's Travel Town as Site of WWII Internment Camp with Sign." April 21, 2023. https://abc7.com/griffith-park-internment-camp-world-war-ii-japanese/13162030.

Ariel, David. "Getty to Return Antiquities to Italy." *Forbes*, August 1, 2007.

Bahr, Lindsey. "Bruce, the Last 'Jaws' Shark, Docks at the Academy Museum." *Opelika-Auburn News*, November 23, 2020. https://web.archive.org/web/20201202051922/https://oanow.com/news/national/bruce-the-last-jaws-shark-docks-at-the-academy-museum/article_465a4404-9f17-597a-9085-3b0a47a38aec.html.

Boehm, Mike. "African American Museum Director Charmaine Jefferson Steps Down." *Los Angeles Times*, July 18, 2014. https://www.latimes.com/entertainment/arts/culture/la-et-cm-california-african-american-museum-charmaine-jefferson-director-20140717-story.html.

Bream, Jon, and Ken Viste. "Museum in a Minute: Grammy Museum Strikes a Chord." *San Jose Mercury News*, April 16, 2009. https://web.archive.org/web/20160303200913/http://www.mercurynews.com/travel/ci_12158930.

Broder, John M. "Observatory Reopens in Fall." *New York Times*, May 11, 2006. https://www.nytimes.com/2006/05/11/us/11griffith.html?ex=1305000000&en=f60234082750651&ei=5088&partner=rssnyt&emc=rss.

Campbell, Sara, C. Knoke and G. Williams. *Handbook of the Norton Simon Museum*. Norton Simon Museum, 2003.

Cooper, Arnie. "Neon Museum Casts Its Otherworldly Glow." *Wall Street Journal*, September 3, 2008. https://www.wsj.com/articles/SB122039501175292599.

Coplans. John. "Pasadena's Collapse and the Simon's Takeover. Diary of a Disaster." Artforum, February 1975. https://www.artforum.com/print/197502/pasadena-s-collapse-and-the-simon-takeover-diary-of-a-disaster-37307.

Cotter, Holland. "Review: The Broad Is an Old-Fashioned Museum for a New Gilded Age." *New York Times*, September 12, 2015. https://www.nytimes.com/2015/09/13/arts/design/review-broad-museum-los-angeles.html.

Duvernoy, Sophie. "10 Oddball L.A. Museums Worth Seeing." *L.A. Weekly*, March 7, 2012. http://www.laweekly.com/arts/10-oddball-la-museums-worth-seeing-2370617#page-2.

Felch, Jason, and Ralph Frammolino. "Getty Lets Her Take Fall, Ex-Curator Says." *Los Angeles Times*, December 29, 2006. http://www.latimes.com/news/local/la-me-true29dec29,0,3427365.story?coll=la-home-headlines.

Flomberg, Deb. "The Bhagavad-Gita Museum: Tour This Fascinating and Educational Museum." *CBS Los Angeles*, July 8, 2013. https://web.archive.org/web/20180311141108/http://losangeles.cbslocal.com/2013/07/08/the-bhagavad-gita-museum-tour-this-fascinating-and-educational-museum.

Gelt, Jessica. "NEA Helps the Autry Museum Provide a Rare Platform for Native American Playwrights." *Los Angeles Times*, March 27, 2017. https://www.latimes.com/entertainment/arts/la-et-cm-nea-native-voices-autry-20170327-story.html.

Gray, Tim. "Shirley Temple Family Gives $5 Million to Academy Museum." *Variety*, October 8, 2015. https://variety.com/2015/film/awards/shirley-temple-family-gives-5-million-to-academy-museum-1201614038.

Greenberger, Alex. "L.A. Moca Elects Hard Rock Café Founder Peter Morton as Trustee." ArtNews, June 23, 2016. http://www.artnews.com/2016/06/23/l-a-moca-elects-hard-rock-cafe-founder-peter-morton-as-trustee.

Griffith Observatory. "History of Griffith Observatory." https://www.griffithobservatory.org/about/history.html.

Hall, Carla. "Elephants Unpack Their Trunks," *Los Angeles Times*, December 17, 2010. http://articles.latimes.com/2010/dec/17/local/la-me-elephants-20101217.

Hauck, Dennis William. *Haunted Places: The National Directory: Ghostly Abodes, Sacred Sites, UFO Landings, and Other Supernatural Locations*. Penguin, 2002.

Hawthorne, Christopher. "Petersen Automotive Museum's New Look Conveys a Happily Tasteless Exterior." *Los Angeles Times*, December 3, 2015. http://www.latimes.com/entertainment/arts/la-et-cm-petersen-automotive-museum-review-20151124-column.html.

Hurlin, Tara. "The Petersen Automotive Museum Presents 'We Are Porsche,' Its Largest Porsche Exhibit Yet." Hemmings, April 18, 2023. https://www.hemmings.com/stories/the-petersen-automotive-museum-presents-we-are-porsche.

King, Kate. "Grammy Museum to Open Newark Location This Fall." *Wall Street Journal*, February 7, 2017. https://www.wsj.com/articles/grammy-museum-to-open-newark-location-this-fall-1486443600.

King, Susan. "Hal Roach's Film Legacy Explored in Hollywood Museum Exhibition." *Los Angeles Times*, July 16, 2014. http://www.latimes.com/entertainment/classichollywood/la-et-classic-hollywood-hal-roach-hollywood-msueum-20140727-story.html.

Levick, Melba, and Stanley Young. *The Big Picture: Murals of Los Angeles*. Little, Brown, and Company, 1988.

Matsuda, Michael. "The Martial Arts History Museum: How It All Began." Martial Arts History Museum, October 25, 2014. https://www.amazon.com/Martial-Arts-History-Museum-Story/dp/1502966964/ref=sr_1_4?ie=UTF8&qid=1454202907&sr=8-4&keywords=martial+arts+history+museum.

Mills, Michelle. "25 Must-See Museums You Have to Visit." *Whittier Daily News*, January 28, 2016. http://www.whittierdailynews.com/arts-and-entertainment/20160128/25-must-see-museums-you-have-to-visit?source=most_viewed.

Miranda, Carolina. "Citing 'Devastating Pandemic,' Academy Museum Once Again Delays Opening—to April 2021." *Los Angeles Times*, June 15, 2020. https://www.latimes.com/entertainment-arts/story/2020-06-15/academy-museum-of-motion-pictures-delays-again-until-april-2021.

Natural History Museum. "Opening New Doors to Natural History." https://nhmlac.org/nhm-commons.

Ng, David. "Hammer Museum to Offer Free Admission Starting Sunday." *Los Angeles Times*, February 7, 2014. https://web.archive.org/web/20160306205120/http://articles.latimes.com/2014/feb/07/entertainment/la-et-cm-hammer-museum-free-admission-sunday-20140207.

Ng, David, and Deborah Vankin. "Works Donated by Artists Raise $22.5 Million for Museum of Contemporary Art in Los Angeles." *Los Angeles Times*, May 13, 2015.

Ng, David, and Jori Finkel. "It's Official: Eli Broad Will Build His Art Museum Downtown; Diller Scofidio + Renfro Will Design." *Los Angeles Times*, August 23, 2010. http://latimesblogs.latimes.com/culturemonster/2010/08/its-official-eli-broad-will-build-his-art-museum-downtown-diller-scofidio-renfro-will-design.html.

O'Toole, Lawrence. "Where Neon Art Comes of Age." *New York Times*, February 4, 1990. https://query.nytimes.com/gst/fullpage.html?res=9C0CE7DE1E3BF937A35751C0A966958260.

Ouroussoff, Nicolai. "The New California Science Center Is a Commanding Presence and Unifying Element at a Neglected Site." *Los Angeles Times*, February 2, 1998. http://articles.latimes.com/1998/feb/02/entertainment/ca-14584.

Pearlman, Robert Z. "End of Year, End of Exhibit: Space Shuttle Endeavour Goes Off View for a Few Years." Space, December 31, 2023. https://www.space.com/space-shuttle-endeavour-exhibit-closing-california-science-center.

Perrottet, Tony. "The Museum of Jurassic Technology: A Throwback to the Private Museums of Earlier Centuries, This Los Angeles Spot Has a True Hodgepodge of Natural History Artifacts." *Smithsonian Magazine* (June 2011). http://www.smithsonianmag.com/arts-culture/Eight-All-American-Curiosities-The-Museum-of-Jurassic-Technology.html.

Purtill, Corinne. "Saving Mt. Wilson Observatory: Inside the Long Battle to Maintain the Spot Where We Found Our Place in the Universe." *Los Angeles Times*, October 3, 2023. https://www.yahoo.com/news/saving-mt-wilson-observatory-inside-100012619.html.

Rothstein, Edward. "A Museum Works to Reinvent Itself, as Well as the American West." *New York Times*, September 22, 2013. https://www.nytimes.com/2013/09/23/arts/design/at-autry-national-center-in-los-angeles-histories-converge.html.

Sanburn, Josh. "Evelyn the Gorilla, Los Angeles." *Time* (March 30, 2011). https://web.archive.org/web/20110115031056/http://www.time.com/time/specials/packages/article/0,28804,2041628_2041646_2041657,00.html.

Serviss, Garrett P. "The Greatest Telescope in the World; Monster Instrument Ordered by Carnegie Institution Will Far Exceed in Power All Other Watchers of the Skies." *New York Times*, January 27, 1907.

Smithsonian Magazine. "California African American Museum | History, Travel, Arts, Science, People, Places." https://www.smithsonianmag.com/museumday/venues/museum/california-african-american-museum.

Stein, Sadie. "Makeup Forever." Paris Review, February 24, 2014. *http*://www.theparisreview.org/blog/2014/02/24/makeup-forever.

Stevens, Doug. "LACMA Then, Now and in the Future Archived." *Los Angeles Times*, April 10, 2015. https://web.archive.org/web/20210928042441/https://www.latimes.com/entertainment/arts/la-ca-g-lacma-campus-20150410-htmlstory.html.

Vankin, Deborah. "Craft & Folk Art Museum Gives Itself a New Name: Craft Contemporary." *Los Angeles Times*, January 15, 2019. https://www.latimes.com/entertainment/arts/la-et-cm-craft-museum-name-change-20190115-story.html.

———. "'Urban Light': Everything You Didn't Know About L.A.'s Beloved Landmark." *Los Angeles Times*, February 14, 2018. http://www.latimes.com/entertainment/arts/la-ca-cm-lacma-urban-light-20180214-htmlstory.html.

Wakim, Marielle. "Fascinating Objects Tell the Story of L.A. in This Revamped Exhibit." *Los Angeles* (May 15, 2018). https://www.lamag.com/culturefiles/becoming-los-angeles.

Weschler, Lawrence. *Mr. Wilson's Cabinet of Wonder: Pronged Ants, Horned Humans, Mice on Toast, and Other Marvels of Jurassic Technology*. Random House, 1995.

Hotels

Bartlett, James. "A Brief History of Downtown's Futuristic Bonaventure Hotel at 40." *LA Weekly*, December 22, 2016. https://www.laweekly.com/a-brief-history-of-downtowns-futuristic-bonaventure-hotel-at-40.

Burk, Margaret T. *Are the Stars Out Tonight?: The Story of the Famous Ambassador and Cocoanut Grove, "Hollywood's Hotel."* Round Table West, 1980.

Chiland, Elijah. "City Gives Developer of Wilshire Grand—LA's Tallest Skyscraper—$60M in Tax Breaks." Curbed LA, March 1, 2017. https://la.curbed.com/2017/3/1/14779348/wilshire-grand-construction-tax-breaks-tallest-tower.

Film Industry Digest. "All of the Academy Awards Venues So Far." June 26, 2020. http://www.filmindustrydigest.com/academy-awards-venues.

Fisher, Eliza. "Beverly Hills Hotel Is Historic Landmark: Iconic Hotel Named First Historic Landmark in Beverly Hills." *Huffington Post*, June 27, 2012. http://www.huffingtonpost.com/2012/06/27/beverly-hills-hotel-historic-landmark_n_1631534.html.

Gomes, Mayra Dias. "THR's Guide to L.A.'s Most Haunted Locations." *Hollywood Reporter*, October 11, 2013. http://www.hollywoodreporter.com/news/haunted-locations-los-angeles-hollywood-645040.

Goodwin, Christopher. "Hollywood Babylon." *Sunday Times Magazine* (November 28, 2010). https://web.archive.org/web/20140202111342/http://www.thesundaytimes.co.uk/sto/Magazine/Features/article452549.ece.

Hodenfield, Chris. "Tales of the Chateau." *Los Angeles Times*, September 14, 1986.

Hoye, Daniel. "Art Deco Los Angeles." *Los Angeles Conservancy*, 1988.

Jameson, Fredric. *Postmodernism, or, the Cultural Logic of Late Capitalism*. Duke University Press, 1991.

Lewis, Randy. "Whitney Houston Was to Attend Clive Davis' Party Tonight." *Los Angeles Times*, February 11, 2012. http://latimesblogs.latimes.com/lanow/2012/02/whitney-houston-clive-davis.html.

Los Angeles Times. "Coveted Beverly Hills Property Sold for $148.3 Million." October 6, 2010. https://www.latimes.com/archives/la-xpm-2010-oct-06-la-fi-9900-wilshire-20101006-story.html.

———. "Pioneer Film Man D.W. Griffith Dies." July 24, 1948.

McFadden, Robert D. "John Belushi, Manic Comic of TV and Films Dies." *New York Times*, March 6, 1982. https://www.nytimes.com/1982/03/06/obituaries/john-belushi-manic-comic-of-tv-and-films-dies.html.

Meares, Hadley. "Off the Boulevard of Broken Dreams: The Knickerbocker Hotel's Haunted History." PBS Socal, June 19, 2015. https://www.pbssocal.org/history-society/off-the-boulevard-of-broken-dreams-the-knickerbocker-hotels-haunted-history.

Mulchin, Chad. "WeHo's 'Riot House' and 4 Reasons You Really Should Have Been There." Wehoville, September 5, 2013. https://www.wehoville.com/2013/09/05/wehos-riot-house-4-reasons-really.

Nichols, Chris. "Movies Filmed at the Ambassador Hotel." *Los Angeles Magazine* (January 22, 2014). http://www.lamag.com/askchris/video-village-with-ask-chris-movies-filmed-at-the-ambassador-hotel.

Pedersen, Erik. "Chateau Marmont Owner Looks to Convert Landmark L.A. Hotel Into Private Club by Year's End." Deadline, July 29, 2020. https://deadline.com/2020/07/chateau-marmont-owner-looks-to-convert-landmark-l-a-hotel-into-private-club-by-years-end-1202998047.

Ryon, Ruth. "Fate of Old Buildings Has No Certainty: Glamorous Past Doesn't Prevent Neglect, Razing" *Los Angeles Times*, May 12, 1985. https://www.latimes.com/archives/la-xpm-1985-05-12-re-18840-story.html.

Salewicz, Chris. "Thin Lizzy's Phil Lynott: 'I Am Johnny Cool, You Know'—a Classic Interview from the Vaults." *Guardian*, September 18, 2012. https://www.theguardian.com/music/2012/sep/18/thin-lizzy-phil-lynott-interview.

Saviss, Ramona. "Coronavirus: The Beverly Hills Hotel and Hotel Bel Air to Donate Food to Medical Personnel." *Hollywood Reporter*, March 24, 2020. https://www.hollywoodreporter.com/lifestyle/style/beverly-hills-hotel-hotel-bel-air-donate-food-medical-personnel-1286330.

Smith, Jack. "The Glory that Was Hollywood Before It Became Hollyweird Returns to the Hollywood Roosevelt Hotel." *Los Angeles Times*, February 4, 1986. http://articles.latimes.com/1986-02-04/news/vw-4310_1_hollywood-boulevard.

Truhler, Kimberly. "The Millennium Biltmore Hotel: The Story of an LA Icon." Discover Los Angeles, March 25, 2021. https://www.discoverlosangeles.com/hotels/the-millennium-biltmore-hotel-the-story-of-an-la-icon.

Yamato, Jen. "Inside the Beverly Hilton, the Home of the Golden Globes and the Hardest Working Hotel in Hollywood." *Los Angeles Times*, January 20, 2017.

https://www.latimes.com/entertainment/movies/la-ca-mn-beverly-hilton-hotel-20170109-story.html.

Yen, Brigham. "Breaking News: Downtown LA's New Landmark Tower, Wilshire Grand, to Become West Coast's Tallest." *DTLA Rising*, February 7, 2013. https://brighamyen.com/2013/02/07/renderings-revealed-new-1100-foot-wilshire-grand-tower-in-downtown-los-angeles.

Film, TV and Music

Andreeva, Nellie. "'The Price Is Right' to Move Production After 5 Decades as Television City Renovations Displace Several Long-Running Series." Deadline, March 8, 2023. https://deadline.com/2023/03/the-price-is-right-move-production-television-city-renovations-1235283050.

CBS News. "Best Studio Tours in Los Angeles," February 25, 2018. https://losangeles.cbslocal.com/2018/02/25/best-studio-tours-in-los-angeles.

Cogan, Jim, and William Clark. *Temples of Sound: Inside the Great Recording Studios*. Chronicle Books, 2003.

Conejo Valley Guide. "MASH Set at Malibu Creek State Park Survives the Woolsey Fire." December 22, 2018. https://www.conejovalleyguide.com/welcome/mash-set-at-malibu-creek-state-park-survives-the-woolsey-fire.

Finke, Nikki. "Kodak Theatre—Oscars Keeps Home at Hollywood & Highland in Newly Named Dolby Theatre." Deadline Hollywood, May 1, 2012. https://www.deadline.com/2012/05/oscars-to-stay-at-hollywood-highland-in-newly-names-dolby-theatre.

Gabler, Neal. *Walt Disney: The Triumph of the American Imagination*. Random House, 2007.

Gelt, Jessica. "Commentary: Sunset Sound Is One of the Last Great L.A. Recording Studios. To Lose It Would Be a Disaster." *Los Angeles Times*, February 20, 2024. https://www.latimes.com/entertainment-arts/story/2024-02-20/the-last-gasps-of-the-great-los-angeles-recording-studios.

Gennawey, Sam. *JayBangs: How Jay Stein, MCA, and Universal invented the Modern Theme Park and Beat Disney at Its Own Game*. Theme Park Press 2016.

Guitar Center. "List of All the Rockwalk/Inductees." Via WebArchive. https://web.archive.org/web/20100928050734/http://www.rockwalk.com/inductees.

Hamedy, Saba. "Sony Pictures Condemns WikiLeaks' Release of Hacked Material." *Los Angeles Times*, April 16, 2015. https://www.latimes.com/entertainment/envelope/cotown/la-et-ct-wikileaks-sony-hack-20150416-story.html.

Hebert, Ray. "City's 58th: Old Chaplin Studio Now Historic Site." *Los Angeles Times*, February 6, 1969.

Hess, John P. "The True Hollywood Story of the Vasquez Rocks—Hollywood's Favorite Rocky Set." FilmmakerIQ, June 21, 2012. https://web.archive.org/web/20200803150032/http://filmmakeriq.com/2012/06/the-true-hollywood-story-of-the-vasquez-rocks-hollywoods-favorite-rocky-set.

Hibbard, James. "Certain Westworld Sets Burn Down in California Wildfire." *Entertainment Weekly* (November 9, 2018). https://ew.com/tv/2018/11/09/westworld-sets-burn.

James, Meg. "CBS Television City Moves Closer to Receiving Historical Landmark Designation." *Los Angeles Times*, May 4, 2018. http://www.latimes.com/business/hollywood/la-fi-ct-cbs-television-city-historic-landmark-20180504-story.html.

Kahlenberg, Richard. "Looking and Listening." *Los Angeles Times*, November 13, 1998. http://articles.latimes.com/1998/nov/13/local/me-42497.

Kilday, Gregg, and Ben Svetkey. "1935–1940—Life in the Foxhole: Insiders Recall 83 Years of Scandal and Stardom at 20th Century Fox." *Hollywood Reporter*, August 2, 2018. https://www.hollywoodreporter.com/lists/a-look-at-83-years-20th-century-fox-1131133/item/eulogy-a-studio-1935-1940-1131136.

Lacher, Irene. "He's a Walking Encyclopedia of Warners History." *Los Angeles Times*, November 5, 1994. https://articles.latimes.com/1994-11-05/entertainment/ca-59059_1_dick-mason.

Lewis, Randy. "How Vasquez Rocks, L.A.'s Onetime Outlaw Hideout, Became 'Star Trek's' Favorite Alien Landscape." *Los Angeles Times*, September 8, 2016. https://www.latimes.com/entertainment/tv/la-et-st-star-trek-50-vasquez-rocks-20160829-snap-story.html.

Los Angeles Business Journal. "Henson Moving to Historical Charlie Chaplin Studios." http://www.thefreelibrary.com/Henson+Moving+to+historical+Charlie+Chaplin+Studios.-a060371488.

Martin, Hugo. "Golden Milestone for the Hollywood Walk of Fame." *Los Angeles Times*, February 8, 2010. https://web.archive.org/web/20190324223751/https://www.latimes.com/archives/la-xpm-2010-feb-06-la-fi-walk-of-fame6-2010feb06-story.html.

Masters, Nathan. "L.A.'s Changing Skyline: A Brief History of Skyscrapers in the City of Angels." KCET, May 23, 2012. http://www.kcet.org/updaily/socal_focus/history/la-as-subject/las-changing-skyline-a-brief-history-of-skyscrapers-in-the-city-of-angels.html.

Morino, Marianne. *The Hollywood Walk of Fame.* Ten Speed Press, 1987.

Myers, Marc. "The Truth About the Tower." *Wall Street Journal*, October 6, 2021. https://www.wsj.com/articles/the-truth-about-the-tower-1479505726.

Newton, Jim. "Mayor Leads a Hurray for Hollywood." *Los Angeles Times*, April 3, 1998. https://articles.latimes.com/1998/apr/03/local/me-35558.

Nolan, A.M. *Rock 'N' Roll Road Trip: The Ultimate Guide to the Sites, the Shrines, and the Legends Across America*. Pharos Books 1992.

O'Connell, Mikey. "HGTV Flips 'Brady Bunch' House, Lists It for $5.5M (Exclusive)." *Hollywood Reporter*, May 24, 2023. https://www.hollywoodreporter.com/tv/tv-news/hgtv-selling-brady-bunch-house-renovations-pictures-1235499038.

Oesterle, Joe. *Weird Hollywood: Your Travel Guide to Hollywood's Local Legends and Best Kept Secrets*. Sterling Publishing 2010.

O'Kane, Caitlin. "Iconic 'Brady Bunch' House for Sale After Nearly 50 Years." CBS News, July 19, 2018. https://www.cbsnews.com/news/iconic-brady-bunch-house-for-sale-after-nearly-50-years.

Pool, Bob. "A Haven for Children in L.A. Closes After 125 Years." *Los Angeles Times*, December 20, 2005. https://www.latimes.com/archives/la-xpm-2005-dec-20-me-hollygrove20-story.html.

Ridenour, Al. "A Chamber of Secrets." *Los Angeles Times*, May 2, 2002. https://web.archive.org/web/20150922112755/http://articles.latimes.com/2002/may/02/news/lv-masons2/2.

Rothel, David. *Ambush of Ghosts: A Guide to Great Western Film Locations*. Empire Publishing, 1991.

Saad, Nardine. "'Jimmy Kimmel' Anniversary Show Invites Debut Guests Snoop, Clooney (Sorry, Matt Damon)." *Los Angeles Times*, January 27, 2023. https://www.latimes.com/entertainment-arts/tv/story/2023-01-27/jimmy-kimmel-live-20-year-anniversary-matt-damon-snoop-dogg.

Schenden, Laurie. "The Hills Are Alive with Plenty to Do." *Los Angeles Times*, September 7, 2000. http://articles.latimes.com/2000/sep/07/entertainment/ca-16838.

Smith, Amber. "Los Angeles Film School: Where Hollywood Grows." Screen Junkies, October 24, 2011. http://www.screenjunkies.com/movies/movie-lists/los-angeles-film-school-where-hollywood-grows.

Solly, Meilan. "100 Years of Hollywood History Lost as California Inferno Destroys Paramount Ranch." *Smithsonian Magazine* (November 12, 2018). https://www.smithsonianmag.com/smart-news/100-years-hollywood-history-lost-california-inferno-razes-paramount-ranch-180970785.

Szalai, Georg, and Paul Bond. "Disney Closes $71.3 Billion Fox Deal, Creating Global Content Powerhouse." *Hollywood Reporter*, March 20, 2019. https://www.

hollywoodreporter.com/news/general-news/disney-closes-fox-deal-creating-global-content-powerhouse-1174498.

Worldwide Guide to Movie Locations. "Pretty Woman." https://movie-locations.com/movies/p/Pretty-Woman.php.

Entertainment

Coates, Chris. "Dimming Disney Hall; Gehry's Glare Gets Buffed." Los Angeles Downtown News, March 21, 2005. http://www.ladowntownnews.com/news/dimming-disney-hall/article_25f5eec5-339b-5f51-810e-1f1af7fcd361.html.

Concepción, Mariel. "Comedian Michael 'Kramer' Richards Goes into Racial Tirade, Banned from Laugh Factory." Newswire, November 20, 2006. Via WebArchive. https://web.archive.org/web/20061231201005/http://www.vibe.com/news/news_headlines/2006/11/comedian_michael_kramer_richards_goes_into_racial_tirade.

D'Alessandro, Anthony. "Netflix Closes Deal of Egyptian Theater; Joining Forces with American Cinematheque." Deadline, May 29, 2020. https://deadline.com/2020/05/netflix-closes-deal-american-cinematheque-egyptian-theatre-1202946525.

Davis, Laura E. "Throwback Thursday: The Story Behind Stars' Handprints in Hollywood." *Los Angeles Times*, March 13, 2014. https://www.latimes.com/nation/la-xpm-2014-mar-13-la-sh-throwback-thursday-stars-handprints-hollywood-chinese-theatre-20140312-story.html.

Discover Los Angeles. "Hollywood Pantages Theatre: The Story of an L.A. Icon." March 14, 2019. https://www.discoverlosangeles.com/things-to-do/hollywood-pantages-theatre-the-story-of-an-la-icon.

Dunham, Elisabeth. "Laughing on the Outside: Rival Comedy Clubs Get Serious in Quest for Patrons." *Los Angeles Times*, May 21, 1987. https://www.latimes.com/archives/la-xpm-1987-05-21-vw-1522-story.html.

Epting, Chris. *Marilyn Monroe Dyed Here: More Locations of America's Pop Culture Landmarks*. Santa Monica Press, 2004.

Fulmer, Melinda. "Disney Unit Buys Historic Masonic Temple." *Los Angeles Times*, July 17, 1998. http://articles.latimes.com/1998/jul/17/business/fi-4422.

Hochman, Steve, "James Taylor and Carole King: They've Still Got Friends.," *Los Angeles Times*, November 30, 2007. http://articles.latimes.com/2007/nov/30/entertainment/et-taylor30.

Hurwitz, Matt. "The Hollywood Bowl: A Unique Blend of Natural Acoustics and Amplified Sound." Mix, October 2014. https://www.mixonline.com/

recording/hollywood-bowl-unique-blend-natural-acoustics-and-amplified-sound-366566.

Lewinski, John Scott. "Quentin Tarantino Saves L.A. Theater." *Hollywood Reporter*, February 18, 2010. https://www.hollywoodreporter.com/news/general-news/quentin-tarantino-saves-la-theater-20854.

Lord, Rosemary. *Los Angeles: Then and Now*. Thunder Bay Press 2002.

Martino, Alison. "The Viper Room Turns 21." LAmag, August 11, 2014. https://lamag.com/music/the-viper-room-turns-21.

Masters, Nathan. "Chavez Ravine: Community to Controversial Real Estate." KCET, September 13, 2012. Via WebArchive. https://web.archive.org/web/20170803015001/https://www.kcet.org/shows/lost-la/chavez-ravine-community-to-controversial-real-estate.

McLellan, Dennis. "Elmer Valentine, Co-Founder of Whisky a Go Go, Dies at 85." *Los Angeles Times*, December 7, 2008. http://www.latimes.com/news/obituaries/la-me-valentine7-2008dec07,0,3236736.story.

McNary, Sharon. "Clash of Billionaires: How Inglewood Got SoFi Stadium and the Super Bowl." LAist, January 27, 2022. https://laist.com/news/los-angeles-activities/nfl-rams-clash-of-billionaires-how-inglewood-got-sofi-stadium-and-the-super-bowl.

Ogden, Tom. "The Comedy Store." In *The Complete Idiot's Guide to Ghosts and Hauntings*. Alpha Books, 1999.

Oliver, Myrna. "Doug Weston, Troubadour Founder, Dies." *Los Angeles Times*, February 15, 1999. http://articles.latimes.com/1999/feb/15/local/me-8369.

Ortiz, Aimee. "Kobe Bryant Is Honored at the Grammys with Tributes and Jerseys." *New York Times*, January 26, 2020. https://www.nytimes.com/2020/01/26/arts/music/grammys-kobe-bryant.html.

Ponsford, Matthew. "Los Angeles to Build World's Most Expensive Stadium Complex." CNN, January 19, 2016. http://edition.cnn.com/style/article/new-nfl-stadium-los-angeles/index.html.

Reich, Howard. "Herb Alpert at 80: Gently Upbeat." *Chicago Tribune*, September 29, 2015. https://www.chicagotribune.com/entertainment/music/reich/ct-jazz-herb-alpert-ent-0930-20150929-column.html.

Romano, Tricia. "Reviving the Roxy: Can the Strip Follow?" *New York Times*, December 4, 2009. https://www.nytimes.com/2009/12/06/fashion/06adler.html.

Rourke, Mary. "Sherman Torgan, 63; Turned an L.A. Adult Movie House into a Haven for Classic and Indie Films." *Los Angeles Times*, July 21, 2007. https://articles.latimes.com/2007/jul/21/local/me-torgan21.

Saperstein, Pat. "Viper Room Sold on Sunset Strip; Site Could Be Redeveloped." *Variety*, August 3, 2018. https://variety.com/2018/music/news/viper-room-sunset-strip-sold-1202894246.

Scher, Valerie. "Disney Hall Opens with a Bang." *San Diego Union-Tribune*, October 25, 2003. http://www.signonsandiego.com/news/features/20031025-9999_1c25gala.html.

Swed, Mark. "Commentary: What the Hollywood Bowl's Complicated History Reveals About Los Angeles." *Los Angeles Times*, June 2, 2022. https://www.latimes.com/entertainment-arts/story/2022-06-02/commentary-hollywood-bowl-2022-history-los-angeles.

Verrier, Richard. "China Firm Buys Naming Rights to Grauman's Chinese Theatre." *Los Angeles Times*, January 11, 2013. http://www.latimes.com/entertainment/envelope/cotown/la-fi-ct-chinese-theater-20130111,0,1298028.story.

Wheeler, Stacie. "50 Years of Dodger Stadium." Dodgers Way, January 22, 2012. https://web.archive.org/web/20171025075440/https://dodgersway.com/2012/01/22/50-years-of-dodger-stadium-the-vision.

Whipp, Glenn. "We Take an Exclusive Tour of Hollywood's Restored Egyptian Theatre, Opening This Fall." *Los Angeles Times*, August 30, 2023. https://www.latimes.com/entertainment-arts/movies/story/2023-08-30/egyptian-theatre-reopening-first-look-netflix-fall-preview.

Young, Jabari. "Crypto.com Buys Naming Rights to Lakers' Staples Center in a $700 Million Deal." CNBC, November 17, 2021. https://www.cnbc.com/2021/11/17/cryptocom-buys-naming-rights-to-lakers-staples-center-in-a-700-million-deal-.html.

Zauzmer, Emily. "'Everybody from Starland Was There': The Hollywood Red Carpet Movie Premiere Turns 100." *Hollywood Reporter*, October 18, 2022. https://www.hollywoodreporter.com/movies/movie-news/robin-hood-1922-movie-premiere-1235242865.

Dining and Shopping

Ajaka, Nadine. "The Man Behind 'The Last Bookstore.'" *The Atlantic*, August 18, 2016. https://www.theatlantic.com/video/index/495605/the-man-behind-the-last-bookstore.

Babayan, Siran. "Guns N' Roses: Appetite for Pastrami." *LA Weekly*, March 7, 2008. http://www.laweekly.com/music/guns-n-roses-appetite-for-pastrami-2152404.

Balla, Lesley. "Musso & Frank Turns 100 as David Lynch, John Travolta and More Dish on Hollywood's Oldest Restaurant: 'There Must Be a Trillion Stories.'" *Hollywood Reporter*, February 22, 2019. https://www.hollywoodreporter.com/features/musso-frank-turns-100-john-travolta-more-tell-all-oral-history-1186746.

Chifalu, Nikki Overfelt. "This Restaurant Introduced Fettuccine Alfredo to the US." TastingTable, March 13, 2023. https://www.tastingtable.com/898478/this-restaurant-introduced-fettuccine-alfredo-to-the-us.

Davis, Genie. "The Friendly Frolic Room." Hollywood Partnership. https://hollywoodpartnership.com/post/friendly-frolic-room.

DeJesus, Erin. "Watch Anthony Bourdain Extoll the Virtues of In-N-Out Burger." Eater, January 8, 2015. http://www.eater.com/2015/1/8/7518215/watch-anthony-bourdain-extoll-the-virtues-of-in-n-out-burger.

Elliot, Farley, and Wonho Frank Lee. "LA Legend Tail O' the Pup Is Serving Hot Dogs Once Again." LA Eater, July 8, 2022. https://la.eater.com/2022/7/8/23200635/tail-o-the-pup-hot-dog-stand-los-angeles-history-hotdog-reopening-news-west-hollywood-photos.

Friedlander, Whitney. "Go on a SoCal Hunt for Googie Architecture." *Baltimore Sun*, May 18, 2008. http://www.baltimoresun.com/travel/la-trw-googie18-2008may18,0,7267506.story?page=1.

Funko. "Grand Opening of Funko Hollywood Set for November 18, 2019." Press release, October 4, 2019. https://investor.funko.com/news-and-events/press-releases/Press-Releases/2019/Grand-Opening-of-Funko-Hollywood-Set-ForNovember-18-2019/default.aspx.

Hess, Alan. "The Oldest McDonald's as Architecture." August 14, 2013. http://alanhess.blogspot.sg/2013/08/the-oldest-mcdonalds-as-architecture.html.

Howser, Huell, prod. "Yamashiro—Visiting (938)." KCET. https://blogs.chapman.edu/huell-howser-archives/2017/03/03/yamashiro-visiting-938.

Kellogg, Carolyn. "Downtown L.A.'s the Last Bookstore Defies Trends." *Los Angeles Times*, June 15, 2011. http://www.latimes.com/books/la-et-last-bookstore-20110615-story.html.

Khouri, Andrew. "Transformation in Store for L.A.'s Historic Core." *Los Angeles Times*, April 2, 2015. http://www.latimes.com/business/realestate/la-fi-property-report-historic-core-20150402-story.html.

Last One on the Bus. "L.A.'s Exotic Yamashiro: Hollywood History with a Spectacular View." November 7, 2021. http://last1onthebus.com/l-a-s-exotic-yamashiro-hollywood-history-with-a-spectacular-view.

Linthicum, Kate, and David Zahniser. "Developer Caruso Again Decides to Bow Out of L.A. Mayoral Race." *Los Angeles Times*, October 12, 2012. https://www.latimes.com/local/la-xpm-2012-oct-12-la-me-1012-caruso-20121012-story.html.

Los Angeles Times. "Rodeo Drive—It's 'A Giant Sundae' and Some of the World's Most Exclusive Shops." *Los Angeles Times*, November 25, 1977.

Martin, Hugo. "Hollywood Fame on a Bun." *Los Angeles Times*, June 7, 2009. https://www.latimes.com/archives/la-xpm-2009-jun-07-fi-himi-pink7-story.html.

National Park Service. "National Register Information System." July 9, 2010. https://npgallery.nps.gov/NRHP.

Ngo, Audrey. "Why L.A.'s Citadel Looks Like an Ancient Assyrian Palace." LAist, June 20, 2018. https://laist.com/2018/06/20/why_las_citadel_looks_like_an_ancie.php.

Nguyen, Daisy. "Rodeo Drive Gets Needed Makeover." *Augusta Chronicle*, December 24, 2003. http://www.lexisnexis.com/hottopics/lnacademic/?verb=sr&csi=156942&sr=HLEAD(RODEO%20DRIVE%20GETS%20NEEDED%20MAKEOVER)%20and%20date%20is%202003.

Nichols, Chris. "L.A. Moves to Protect Vintage Mom and Pop Shops." *Los Angeles Magazine* (March 11, 2024). https://lamag.com/news/los-angeles-to-protect-vintage-mom-and-pop-shops-grants.

———. "Randy's Donuts Says It's Been Famous Since '62. History Tells a Different Story." *Los Angeles Magazine* (June 4, 2021). https://www.lamag.com/askchris/ask-chris-randys-donuts.

———. "Review: After 70 Years, the Norms Chain of Iconic Googie Diners Looks to the Future." *Los Angeles Magazine* (October 17, 2019). https://www.lamag.com/digestblog/norms-70-breakfast.

The Original Farmers Market Map and Visitors Guide. June 2008.

Perman, Stacy. *In-N-out Burger: A Behind-the-Counter Look at the Fast-Food Chain that Breaks All the Rules*. Collins Business, 2009.

Podsada, Janice. "Funko, the Everett-Based Toymaker, Opens a Hollywood Store." *Everett Herald*, November 18, 2019. https://www.heraldnet.com/business/funko-the-everett-based-toymaker-opens-a-hollywood-store.

Sanchez, Jesus. "Farmers Market to Unveil New Development." *Los Angeles Times*, May 22, 1998. http://articles.latimes.com/1998/may/22/local/me-52392.

Sandomir, Richard. "Mario Maglieri, Who Coddled Rockers at His Clubs, Dies at 93." *New York Times*, May 11, 2017. https://www.nytimes.com/2017/05/09/arts/music/mario-maglieri-dead-ran-whisky-a-go-go.html.

Scattergood, Amy. "Catcher and the Deli Rye." *Los Angeles Times*, April 9, 2008. http://articles.latimes.com/2008/apr/09/food/fo-journal9.

Solmonson, Lesley. "Lights, Camera…Cocktails! Five Historic Bars from Hollywood's Golden Age." *Smithsonian Magazine* (February 23, 2017). https://www.smithsonianmag.com/travel/relive-hollywoods-golden-age-these-five-historic-los-angeles-bars-180962286.

Stoelik, Dave. "Second-Hand Store Sells Hollywood Hand-Me-Downs." Spectrum News, October 19, 2022. https://spectrumnews1.com/ca/la-west/entertainment/2022/10/19/second-hand-store-sells-hollywood-hand-me-downs.

Venema, Vibeke. "The Donut King Who Went Full Circle—From Rags to Riches, Twice." BBC News, November 28, 2020. https://www.bbc.com/news/stories-54546427.

Vincent, Roger. "They Can't All Be Grand Central Market: Does L.A. Have Too Many Food Halls?" *Los Angeles Times*, September 12, 2019. https://www.latimes.com/business/story/2019-09-11/grand-central-market-food-halls-high-demand.

Wahl, Jan. "From Ru Paul to Tallulah Bankhead, Larry Edmunds Bookshop Is the Place to Be!" *San Francisco Bay Times*, August 26, 2021. https://sfbaytimes.com/from-ru-paul-to-tallulah-bankhead-larry-edmunds-bookshop-is-the-place-to-be.

Waserman, Kastle. "Rock 'n' Rollers, Your Tab Is Running at the Rainbow." *Los Angeles Times*, December 15, 2002.

Willman, Chris. "Amoeba Music: A Look Inside the Sprawling New Hollywood Store." *Variety*, April 1, 2021. https://variety.com/2021/music/news/amoeba-music-new-store-hollywood-location-move-photos-video-1234942264.

Young, Jacy. "LAistory: Tail O' The Pup." LAist, March 28, 2009. https://web.archive.org/web/20200204012313/https://laist.com/2009/03/28/laistory_tail_o_the_pup.php.

Haunted Horror, Scandal and True Crime

Alzayat, Dima. "Cinespia Celebrates Age 10 by Staying Up All Night." *Los Angeles Times*, August 12, 2011. http://www.latimes.com/theguide/events-and-festivals/la-et-guidefeature-20110812,0,3441270.story.

Barcella, Laura. "Has the Black Dahlia Murder Finally Been Solved?" *Rolling Stone* (January 26, 2018). https://web.archive.org/web/20180630220043/https://www.rollingstone.com/culture/features/has-the-black-dahlia-murder-finally-been-solved-w515848.

Barragan, Bianca. "Mapping 13 Key Locations in the 1969 Manson Family Murders." Curbed LA, October 22, 2014. https://la.curbed.com/maps/charles-manson-sharon-tate-prison.

Boehm, Mike. "Museum of Death in L.A. Buys Kevorkian Suicide Device Thanatron." *Los Angeles Times*, July 21, 2014. http://www.latimes.com/entertainment/arts/culture/la-et-cm-jack-kevorkian-museum-of-death-hollywood-thanatron-20140718-story.html.

Burton, Jamie. "American Horror Stories: The Real LA Mansion Used as the Murder House." *Newsweek*, July 15, 2021. https://www.newsweek.com/american-horror-stories-real-la-mansion-murder-house-ahs-rosenheim-1610037.

Chamings, Andrew. "A Hidden Staircase on the California Coast Leads to a Heart-Wrenching Urban Legend." *SFGate*, February 11, 2024. https://www.sfgate.com/la/article/murphy-ranch-nazi-bunker-hike-18649347.php.

———. "Why No One Wants to Live in This $2.4 million California Mansion." *SFGate*, May 5, 2024. https://www.sfgate.com/la/article/no-one-wants-live-in-california-mansion-19429677.php.

Cowan, Jared. "Every Famous Filming Location from John Carpenter's Halloween." *Los Angeles Magazine* (October 12, 2018). https://lamag.com/film/halloween-locations-40.

Di Mambro, Dina. *True Hollywood Noir: Filmland Mysteries and Murders*. Self-published, 2013.

Duke, Alan. "Hotel with Corpse in Water Tank Has Notorious Past." CNN, February 23, 2013. https://www.cnn.com/2013/02/21/us/california-horror-hotel/index.html.

Ehrenreich, Ben. "The End." *Los Angeles Magazine* (November 1, 2010). https://lamag.com/news/the-end.

Epting, Chris. *James Dean Died Here: Locations of America's Pop Culture Landmarks*. Santa Monica Press, 2003.

Fernandez, Alexia. "Manson Murder Spree: All the Hollywood Places Charles Manson's Followers Killed Their Victims." *People* (August 1, 2019). https://people.com/movies/charles-manson-family-crime-map.

Gilmore, John. *Severed: The True Story of the Black Dahlia Murder*. 2nd ed. Amok Books, 2006.

Gumbel, Andrew. "American Times: Hollywood, California, the Doyenne of Death Heads for Tinseltown." *The Independent*, December 8, 1999.

Kolberg, Sharael. "LA Conservationists Are Mad as Hell—Muralist Commissioned to Repaint the Historic Cecil Hotel—Speaks!." *Downtown Los Angeles Weekly*, April 20, 2022. https://dtlaweekly.com/conservationists-muralist-cecil-hotel-signage.

Kudler, Adrian Click. "Michael Jackson Death House Finally Sells for $18.1 Million." Curbed LA, November 5, 2012. https://la.curbed.com/2012/11/5/10312316/michael-jackson-death-house-finally-sells-for-181-million.

Linedecker, Clifford. *OJ A to Z*. St. Martin Press, 1995.

Llewellyn, John F. *Birth of a Cemetery: Forest Lawn Memorial-Park*. Tropico Press, 2018.

Lopez, Steve. "Column: Exclusive West L.A. Property, Surrounded by Stars, on Sale for $745,000. Are You Dying to Move In?" *Los Angeles Times*, May

27, 2020. https://www.latimes.com/california/story/2020-05-27/column-exclusive-west-l-a-plot-surrounded-by-big-stars-on-sale-for-745-000-but-you-gotta-die-to-move-in.

Pollina, Richard. "Beverly Hills Mansion Where Menendez Brothers Murdered Their Parents Sells for Whopping $17M." *New York Post*, March 22, 2024. https://nypost.com/2024/03/22/real-estate/menendez-brothers-mansion-sells-for-17-million-exactly-28-years-after-their-murder-conviction.

Russell, Ron. "Splendor Fades at Final Resting Place of Famous, Almost Famous." *Los Angeles Times*, July 3, 1988. http://articles.latimes.com/1988-07-03/local/me-8717_1_final-resting-places.

Saperstein, Pat, and Matthew Chernov. "21 Spookiest Horror Film and TV Locations Around Los Angeles." *Variety*, October 12, 2020. https://variety.com/lists/horror-film-locations-los-angeles-halloween-poltergeist.

Sounes, Howard. *27: A History of the 27 Club Through the Lives of Brian Jones, Jimi Hendrix, Janis Joplin, Kurt Cobain, and Amy Winehouse*. Tantor and Blackstone Publishing, 2021.

Styles, Seth. "Putting Down the Los Feliz Murder House." *John Hart Real Estate*, April 2, 2023. https://www.johnhartrealestate.com/blog/2023/04/los-feliz-murder-house.

TMZ. "Michael Jackson Dies." June 25, 2009. https://www.tmz.com/2009/06/25/michael-jackson-dies-death-dead-cardiac-arrest.

Wilson, Scott. *Resting Places: The Burial Sites of More than 14,000 Famous Persons*. 3rd ed. McFarland, 2016.

Worldwide Guide to Movie Locations. "A Nightmare on Elm Street." https://movie-locations.com/movies/n/Nightmare-On-Elm-Street-1984.php.

Young, Betty Lou. *Rustic Canyon and the Story of the Uplifters*. Casa Vieja Press, 1975.

Odd LA

Betsky, Aaron. "The 'Witches' Cottage': A Realized Fairy-Tale Fantasy in Beverly Hills." *Los Angeles Times*, December 24, 1992. http://articles.latimes.com/1992-12-24/news/we-3329_1_beverly-hills.

Bonner, Robert C. "L.A.'s Other Oil Fields with Schools Built on Them." *Los Angeles Times*, October 31, 1999. http://articles.latimes.com/1999/oct/31/opinion/op-28210.

Carley, Chris. "Tourists: Don't Accept the Aspiring Big City Music Star's 'Free' CD (Even If They Offer to Autograph It for You." Eye of the Flyer, April 6, 2024. https://eyeoftheflyer.com/2024/04/06/hollywood-blvd-cd-scam.

Eades, Mark. "Memories of Walt Disney's Steam Train from His Daughter." *Orange County Register*, August 20, 2015. https://web.archive.org/web/20170712134953/http://www.ocregister.com/2015/08/20/memories-of-walt-disneys-steam-train-from-his-daughter.

———. "Mine Train that Once Ran at Disneyland Gets a New Home." *Orange County Register*, December 22, 2016. https://web.archive.org/web/20170712135330/http://www.ocregister.com/2016/12/22/mine-train-that-once-ran-at-disneyland-gets-a-new-home.

Elliott, Farley. "Inside the Magic Castle, the Most Mysterious Restaurant in Los Angeles." Eater Los Angeles, July 26, 2017. https://web.archive.org/web/20240102021558/https://la.eater.com/2017/7/26/16021786/magic-castle-hollywood-los-angeles-inside-photos.

Foster, R. Daniel. "L.A.'s Quirkiest Museum? It's Gotta be the Bunny Museum." *Los Angeles Times*, March 22, 2018. https://www.latimes.com/home/la-hm-bunny-museum-20180322-htmlstory.html.

Grigoryants, Olga. "Los Angeles Moves Toward Closing Down the West Pico Drill Site." *Los Angeles Daily News*, December 15, 2023. https://www.dailynews.com/2023/12/14/los-angeles-moves-toward-stopping-the-west-pico-drill-site-in-west-l-a.

Grippa, Cheyenne. "The Paul Smith Pink Wall Instagram Landmark Costs "$60,000 Per Year to Maintain." Los Angeleno, March 8, 2019 https://losangeleno.com/places/paul-smith-instagram-landmark.

Kielbasa, John R. "Rancho La Brea." In *Historic Adobes of Los Angeles County*. Dorrance Publishing Company, 1998.

Kreuzer, Nikki. "Offbeat L.A.: Storybook Architecture in Los Angeles." Los Angeles Beat, February 14, 2013. http://thelosangelesbeat.com/2013/02/offbeat-l-a-storybook-architecture-in-los-angeles.

Kudler, Adrian Glick. "The Story of the Magic Castle, One of the Most LA Places in LA." Curbed LA, January 3, 2013. https://web.archive.org/web/20240102024321/https://la.curbed.com/2013/1/3/10289754/the-story-of-the-magic-castle-one-of-the-most-la-places-in-la.

Lew, Chloe, and Brittany Martin. "Where to Find L.A.'s Most Instagrammed Walls IRL." *Los Angeles Magazine* (August 17, 2017). https://lamag.com/art/where-to-find-l-a-s-most-instagrammed-walls-irl.

Morton, Ella. "Basically Every City in the U.S. Has a Piece of the Berlin Wall." Atlas Obscura, June 22, 2015. https://www.atlasobscura.com/articles/basically-every-city-in-the-u-s-has-a-piece-of-the-berlin-wall.

Page Museum. "About the Museum." Natural History Museum of Los Angeles County Foundation. http://www.tarpits.org/our-story/about-the-page.

Shaw, Joy C. "Bunny Love—Pasadena Couple Collects Only the Cutest (and Don't Call Them Rabbits)." *San Diego Union-Tribune*, February 15, 1999. https://pqasb.pqarchiver.com.

Stephens, E.J., and Marc Wanamaker. *Griffith Park*. Arcadia Publishing, 2011.

Williams, Virginia. "15 Surprising Places to See the Berlin Wall." Mental Floss, August 5, 2021. https://www.mentalfloss.com/article/649045/places-to-see-berlin-wall.

INDEX

C

J

K

L

M

R

S

X

Y

Z

ABOUT THE AUTHOR

Adam Papagan was born in Los Angeles at Cedars-Sinai Hospital. He has lived in Los Angeles his entire life and received a bachelor's degree in anthropology from UCLA. Papagan is the creator of the O.J. Simpson Tour, the *Real Housewives of Beverly Hills* Tour and the *Curb Your Enthusiasm* Tour and has led expeditions across Southern California for thousands of happy customers. In 2021, he ran as a candidate in the gubernatorial recall election on a nonpartisan platform to spread awareness about California's political process. When he's not touring around Los Angeles, Adam resides in the much quieter suburb of Glendale.